THE INNER MARRIAGE

"*The Inner Marriage* is more than an insightful read, I found it to be a perceptive self-development journey that opens the mind into non-dual thinking, teaching us to apply this into our love, work, and family relationships. A must-read for everyone wanting to understand themselves, the nature of reality, and their loved ones better."

~ **KIP ANDERSEN,** producer of Netflix premiere *Seaspiracy* and director of the Netflix documentaries *What the Health* and *Cowspiracy*

"*The Inner Marriage* by Elliott Saxby grants entrance into the long misunderstood realm of feminine and masculine dynamics. It is an insightful jewel for those seeking to bring about growth in their own inner world while developing mature relationships with the opposite sex. The wisdom given has the potential to transform the reader by clearing the smokescreen that many of us are consumed by when trying to understand why we or others behave the way we do. Elliott gives us the motivation and a way to improve by providing a blueprint that is quite accessible and applicable to everyday life. I will return to this book again and again for guidance and reference it in my own teachings. Thank you!"

~ **YOGINI GOPIKA,** traditional tantric yoga teacher

THE INNER MARRIAGE

A Guide to Masculine & Feminine Polarity Work

ELLIOTT SAXBY

FINDHORN PRESS

Findhorn Press
One Park Street
Rochester, Vermont 05767
www.findhornpress.com

Text stock is SFI certified

Findhorn Press is a division of Inner Traditions International

Disclaimer
The information in this book is given in good faith and intended for information only. Neither author nor publisher can be held liable by any person for any loss or damage whatsoever which may arise from the use of this book or any of the information therein.

Cataloging-in-Publication data for this title is available from the Library of Congress

ISBN 978-1-64411-604-3 (print)
ISBN 978-1-64411-605-0 (ebook)

Printed and bound in the United States by Lake Book Manufacturing, Inc. The text stock is SFI certified. The Sustainable Forestry Initiative® program promotes sustainable forest management.

10 9 8 7 6 5 4 3 2 1

Edited by Michael Hawkins
Text design and layout by Anna-Kristina Larsson
This book was typeset in Garamond and Raleway

To send correspondence to the author of this book, mail a first-class letter to the author c/o Inner Traditions • Bear & Company, One Park Street, Rochester, VT 05767, USA and we will forward the communication, or contact the author directly at **https://elliottsaxby.com**

So many people have loved me and hurt me in life.
Some of this pain has led to my greatest gifts and achievements,
while some of the nicest things that people have done for me,
has led to the worst consequences.

Thank you all for teaching me not to judge.
I love you all.

Contents

~

Part 1

The Mature, the Immature, and the Shadow

Part 2

Sex and Other Applications of the Polarity Framework

Part 3

Shadow Work

MAP

Preface

Masculine and Feminine Polarity Work is inspired by many sources, from the present day and stretching back thousands of years, into the Vedas *(sacred knowledge)* and Advaita teachings *(non-dualism)*. This book explores their application in modern life as a framework for self-development and to align our physical, mental, and emotional bodies.

Working with the fundamental building blocks of life, we learn how to move beyond judgements, raise our vibration and use the laws of polarity and duality and vibration and attraction for personal and planetary transformation. Utilizing these universal laws through "Masculine and Feminine Polarity Work", makes them easy to apply in our families, relationships, at work and in a range of therapy, coaching, healthcare, and rehabilitation settings.

This book is not designed to give answers or tell us how to live life. It is designed to help us look at life from a different perspective, bringing in more emotional awareness and helping us to find our own answers.

By understanding evolution, through the concept of polarity and duality in relation to the law of attraction, we recognize the current integration of opposing traits within ourselves. We use our inner masculine and inner feminine dynamics to change, develop and evolve each other: like an inner marriage. As we explore the polarity and duality within ourselves, we come to see that the foundations of life and what holds reality together are paradoxical and forever changing. The more we understand these paradoxical contradictions, the more we come to understand ourselves.

The polarity framework, the core of this book, is an expression of universal law working chaotically and perfectly at the same time. It focuses on the human experience, the values and emotional perspectives that shape us. Its teachings can be seen throughout history, the most obvious expression being the I Ching which explains various life paths and how they interact with each other through the expressions of Yin and Yang, old and young.

The book explains our paradoxical and unsolvable nature and how by embracing our shadow we can come to enjoy life fully, seeing the multi-dimensional nature of our humanity and fundamentally changing our relationship to others and importantly to suffering, sadness, anger and all other emotions that many deem negative. The book looks at life from many facets while always bringing our attention back to the universal laws of polarity and duality and how to apply these laws in all aspects of life.

The polarity framework was inspired by a multitude of sources including the I Ching, Western Tantra teachings and the integral theory. I was using the framework with clients and teaching it before this book was written, seeing the simplicity, power and rapid transformations that came from it on a daily basis. The insights and learnings that came from each client showing up with their vulnerabilities and desires to be better people should take most of the credit for this book, although I have still been influenced by many amazing people throughout life, and the list of recommended material in this book has surely been a gift.

Introduction

⁓

This book serves as a guide, to help you navigate polarity, duality, and your own evolution:

- This book is abstract, giving overlying principles and concepts, that should be coloured with your own life experiences and unique understandings.
- This book is practical, and you can start using the maps contained within it immediately, beginning to change your inner masculine and feminine dynamics.

The four maps can be downloaded and printed from www.polaritywork.com.

1 The Masculine and Feminine Mirror
2 Devolving the Masculine and Feminine
3 Evolving the Masculine and Feminine
4 The Immature's Shadow

They outline how to move between our masculine and feminine polarities in order to evolve ourselves and help others evolve, finding more integration in life by first acknowledging our separation. Glancing at the maps, we might think the point is to move out of our immature values, but it is not. The maps express a constant contradiction of life: in that each time we understand or experience life from one perspective, our understanding of the whole must change. We will come to understand that many of these immature traits are needed and have a healthy expression, such as competition and how often the line between right, wrong, good, and bad is simply a judgement. The maps guide us towards making all expressions of our masculine and feminine healthy, but still allowing in a little darkness and shadow as this is what helps us evolve.

If you only print one, make sure it is, *"The Masculine and Feminine Mirror"*, as this contains all the information in it once *you have learned how to read it.* Use it in self-development, romantic relationships, partnerships, with children, your friends, and colleagues. Use it to manage a business and manage your staff. Every time you notice an immature expression in yourself, take out these maps and see what lessons you can learn by looking at both the polarity and duality of the situation.

It's best to read this book from start to finish, but if you wanted to, you could skip to the *"Physical, Mental & Emotional Bodies"* section and then come back to the *"The Mature, The Immature and The Shadow"*. It is useful to read the Glossary early on as this helps frame concepts as they are used in the book, such as subconscious, unconscious, and collective consciousness.

Remember that our immature traits and values, as described in the maps, are not necessarily *"bad"* but need to be developed. The process is about judging less and coming to a naturally evolving state of health and balance.

A Note . . .

. . . on the Use of Language, Gender, and Not Always Being Politically Correct

Masculine and Feminine Polarity Work, gives us a lens to better understand ourselves, our relationships to others, our relationship to the world, and the dualistic nature of life. By constantly looking at all these relationships through the masculine and feminine lens, we have a powerful framework for personal growth and transformation that ultimately allows us to better integrate as a whole person.

Masculine and Feminine Polarity Work recognizes that we all have an inner masculine and an inner feminine that is not dependent on gender. This book mostly explores life through individuals who identify with the expression connected to their gender: so, a heterosexual masculine man and a heterosexual feminine woman.

However, as you read further you will see how the labels and methods of explaining are not as important as the concepts being conveyed. Terms like he and his, and she and hers, will be used even though masculinity and femininity are not bound by gender. If this triggers a negative reaction in you, try replacing the masculine he, and his, with Yang and feminine she, and hers, with Yin.

Sometimes we will look at situations from the male, masculine perspective, and other times from the female, feminine perspective. Most of the time, it will not matter which way round we use the example: just change it in your head to suit your gender and your personal masculine and feminine preferences.

The concepts discussed can be applied to the eight possible arrangements of masculinity and femininity in couples of the same or different gender. For example:

- a masculine man and a feminine woman;
- a feminine man and masculine woman;
- a masculine man and a feminine man, and so on, and so forth.

15

It also applies to couples, who are balanced and fluid in their expressions of masculinity and femininity, and couples where one partner is well balanced and the other predominantly one way.

Self-development work of this nature is relevant to all individuals, in all types of relationships: we can be gay, straight, bi or lesbian; we can be cis, transgender, third gender, someone who identifies with both genders, gender fluid; we can be intersex. Non-binary or demigender people might find some of the concepts in this book alien but are encouraged to take from it what is useful.

We can change many times in our life, from one predominant way of being to another. Some people and couples might switch between the different expressions several times a month, others might prefer to be in their predominant gender-related expression for most of their life and look for a partner who allows them to be like this, *at least until conflict arises.* This book is not trying to give us labels, put us into boxes, or tell us there is a correct way to be. It allows the duality and polarity of masculinity and femininity to be more transparent, accepting and less dogmatic in each of us. We should use it to support the evolution of our integrated self. A self with its own integrated balance of *masculine, feminine, mature, immature, healthy, unhealthy, and shadow traits:* a self, free of past conditioning and limiting beliefs.

In summary, this book uses gender to define and express qualities and how they play out in relationships. The gender assigned to each quality is only a guide. All emotions and values can be applied with a masculine or feminine energy. This is to say, *you might attach a trait on the maps to be more masculine instead of feminine, your truth is more important than the maps,* the maps are guides to help navigate emotional polarity and the paradoxes of life. Ultimately, we are learning how everything in life is polarity and by having four quadrants instead of two halves by having duality and polarity, it is much easier for us to manage evolution. Masculine and feminine are two very helpful metaphors that support us to physically embody this understanding and to understand ourselves.

Part 1

THE MATURE,
THE IMMATURE,
AND THE SHADOW

The Masculine and Feminine Mirror

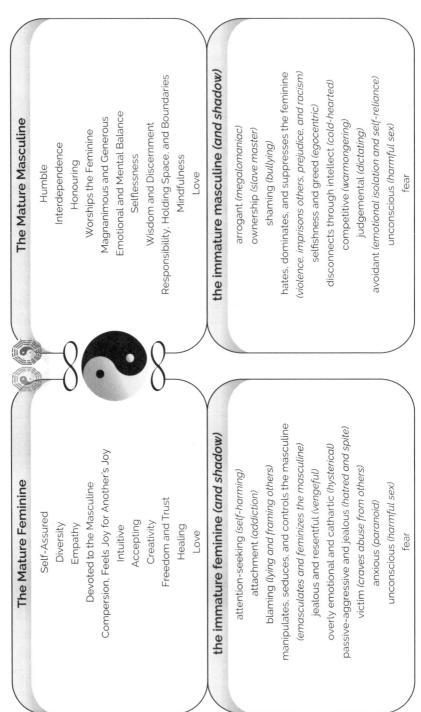

The Mature Feminine

Self-Assured

Diversity

Empathy

Devoted to the Masculine

Compersion. Feels Joy for Another's Joy

Intuitive

Accepting

Creativity

Freedom and Trust

Healing

Love

the immature feminine (and shadow)

attention-seeking (self-harming)

attachment (addiction)

blaming (lying and framing others)

manipulates, seduces, and controls the masculine
(emasculates and feminizes the masculine)

jealous and resentful (vengeful)

overly emotional and cathartic (hysterical)

passive-aggressive and jealous (hatred and spite)

victim (craves abuse from others)

anxious (paranoid)

unconscious (harmful sex)

fear

The Mature Masculine

Humble

Interdependence

Honouring

Worships the Feminine

Magnanimous and Generous

Emotional and Mental Balance

Selflessness

Wisdom and Discernment

Responsibility, Holding Space, and Boundaries

Mindfulness

Love

the immature masculine (and shadow)

arrogant (megalomaniac)

ownership (slave master)

shaming (bullying)

hates, dominates, and suppresses the feminine
(violence, imprisons others, prejudice, and racism)

selfishness and greed (egocentric)

disconnects through intellect (cold-hearted)

competitive (warmongering)

judgemental (dictating)

avoidant (emotional isolation and self-reliance)

unconscious (harmful sex)

fear

Masculine and Feminine traits act as a guide only. Traits, emotions, and values should not be made binary as most can be applied with

1
Moving between the Masculine and the Feminine

~

We all have an inner masculine and inner feminine which is not dependent on gender. Both our masculine and feminine have mature and immature expressions.

If our feminine is in her mature, then our immature masculine will try to bring her down through suppression, control and domination, and if our masculine is in his mature, then our immature feminine will try to bring him down by playing the victim, being the centre of attention, gossiping, manipulating, blaming, and other immature feminine traits.

They can only rise up into their mature expressions together. To bring the immature masculine to his mature, we need to know the mature feminine within ourselves. And to bring the immature feminine to the mature feminine, we need the mature masculine within ourselves. This is very similar to raising children, in that:

- *for a child to step into their mature feminine power, the child needs mature masculine presence within themselves and for this the child needs a model, someone they can take their masculine imprint from, generally a father figure;*
- *but equally important for a child to develop mature masculine presence within themselves, they need love from their mature feminine which they also need a model for, generally a mother figure.*

Similarly, in our partnerships the same dynamic is going on. if we see our partner acting from their immature in an unhealthy way, then we need to embody the opposing mature trait, not the same one that they are in and *not* the opposing immature. By doing this as adults, we are able to take healthy mature imprints of masculinity and femininity (which we are subconsciously doing all of the time) from the people closest to us, in the same way that we hope children do through access to good role models. Thus, no matter our age, we are all constantly learning from and influencing each other whether we like it or not. Learning to use polarity and duality in our life, is learning to evolve our emotional dynamics and traits, so that nearly all our expressions are healthy.

Once we understand how to work with polarity, we no longer need to be afraid of it. Polarity, especially emotional polarity, can be difficult for some people as they create a black and white existence, becoming trapped in judgements of good and bad, right and wrong, happy or sad. The framework gives insights into our pain and suffering so that we can use them as a gift and tool for growth. The key to *not* becoming stuck in polarity is learning to use duality, learning to embody the masculine, and feminine traits and the polarities within them.

Common Traits

What we believe and feel in relation to what is masculine and what is feminine is our truth and no one should take this away from us or tell us that we are wrong. But for the purpose of learning to use the polarity framework, traits have been identified as either masculine or feminine, mature or immature and arranged in a way to support you to see how emotional polarity and behavioral polarity can work, positively or negatively in numerous ways. The labelling is not intended to be definitive but to teach you how to work with the polarity framework in your own way with any and all emotional and behavioral traits that emerge throughout your life.

Our mature masculine is wisdom, intellect, knowledge, and cooperation. It is our safety, our boundaries, our yes and our no. It is discernment and the right application of free will.

Our mature feminine is everything that we enjoy about life. It is beauty, music, dancing, food, and language. It is everything that we can see, taste, touch, smell and hear. It is everything in creation, as well as diversity, empathy, and our intuition. It is our yes for life, a yes with no judgement, no comparison, or thought of good or bad. It is the complete expression and acceptance of all life.

Our immature self creates conflict, but it is this conflict that spurs us on and instigates change, transformation, and our deeper insights. When we can recognize the gifts within our conflict, we will grow, learn, and develop, whether enjoying the process or not.

Our immature self lets us know when something is out of balance and needs attention. By cycling between our mature and immature self with awareness, we develop a healthy ego. A healthy ego makes life beautiful, while allowing us to acknowledge that it is not who we really are. While our unhealthy ego can still create feelings of joy, it is always perpetuating our sense of *"separate self"* through fear and suffering.

Our separate self is best described as: our experience of the world from the mind. Reacting to the world from memories and mental programming, creating fear, and opposition from greed and survival needs, or attacking others from these same places. As we gain more access to empathy, emotional intelligence, intuition, and a sense of the collective consciousness, we come to know that the separate self is a partial truth, not *the* truth.

Fundamentals of the Framework

If we feel we are in our immature feminine, bringing our masculine down, we need to stop and move into our mature masculine's values and traits: looking at *how we are not supporting our feminine*. We need to ask questions like:

- What have I said yes to, that I should have said no to?
- Where have I crossed my own boundaries, or allowed someone else to do so?
- Where does my feminine not feel safe?
- What mental concepts or knowledge have I learned that I am not applying to life?
- And where am I not using discernment to choose the best outcome?

And if we feel our immature masculine is bringing our feminine down then we need to stop and start focusing on our mature feminine's values and attributes in order to bring our masculine up:

- looking to see where inspiration, creativity, and diversity are lacking in our life;
- where we are failing to listen to our intuition;
- where we are not accepting ourselves enough;
- and why we are not feeling self-assured.

Masculine and Feminine Polarity work, or working with polarity and duality in its simplest form is about:

1 embodying the opposing mature pole, to bring the immature up;
2 making our immature healthy;
3 learning from, and transforming our shadows.

When we are able to work with the masculine and feminine polarities within ourselves, developing our ego, navigating between our inner and outer expressions, our mature and immature, and using our shadow as a tool for growth, we come closer to mastering duality.

Practical Examples

Example 1
Attention-Seeking

We are going to use the immature feminine's attention-seeking as an example, believing that everything is about us, thus taking everything personally in a self-obsessed, self-absorbed and selfish way.

The immature feminine's *attention-seeking* opposes the immature masculine's *arrogance*. Relating this to taking everything personally, the masculine will be locked into his state of separation, reaffirming that he and his arrogant beliefs are the correct way. Generally speaking, the more arrogant we are, the more attention-seeking we will be, whether we admit it or not.

To evolve the immature feminine's attention-seeking to her healthy, mature expression of *self-assurance,* we need to embody the trait that opposes it in the mature masculine, which is *humbleness.*

To simply say, "stop seeking attention and then you will be self-assured", is not so easy and is the same as saying, "stop being in your immature feminine and then you will automatically be in your mature feminine", which is generally not true. We normally need to:

- do something;
- learn something;
- or change something to get there.

By becoming the mature humble masculine, we indirectly evolve the immature feminine from attention-seeking into self-assurance. We use both polarity and duality to change or evolve our situation and understanding. So, by stepping into our mature masculine and by being humble, we remove the need for attention-seeking in the feminine, as attention-seeking in the feminine is the lack of humbleness in the masculine.

This does not mean we become less feminine, and more masculine; it simply means that we become more self-assured, and humble.

Trying to change by *not* being something, is much more difficult, and almost impossible, compared to changing something by being something else. Similarly, Albert Einstein (German-born theoretical physicist, 1879 to 1955) said: *"We cannot solve our problems with the same thinking we used when we created them."*

When we use the Masculine and Feminine Polarity Framework to create change, it is clearer to see what we need to do in each quadrant, and this generally is:

- Embody: the opposing mature.
- Evolve: into the mature, of that same polarity.
- Avoid: the opposing immature.

By taking the focus away from the immature quadrant that we are having trouble in, we have a much better chance of evolving it. So, in relation to our example above of attention-seeking in the immature feminine:

- We embody: humbleness (the mature masculine), and all the other, mature masculine traits, that are a fit for us.
- We evolve: into self-assurance (the mature feminine).
- We avoid: arrogance (the immature masculine).

And by doing this, we indirectly stop seeking attention and move out of the immature feminine.

If this sounds complex, then please read it again with the *Masculine and Feminine Polarity Work Maps,* until it becomes clear. This abstract theory is important to learn. The specific traits and labels we assign help, but once we really understand the framework, we will start to apply it in our life without thinking. Our brain will automatically start to think in polarity and duality, healthy and unhealthy, mature and immature. We will indirectly move away from good and bad, right and wrong; you are this, and I am that, and similar judgements.

There are many, and various methods out there to help us make changes and embody qualities within ourselves, including: emotional freedom tapping technique (EFT), self-hypnosis, and basic forms of breathwork. One of the simplest ways is to just start with an intention, write it down, say it to yourself in the morning, meditate on it, go for a massage, to the gym, or a yoga class, and dedicate that session to your intention. Imagine your life once this intention is your reality.

The hard part is learning our lessons within the polarities that we are working with, as everyone's journey is unique, and often, so are our lessons. It is not wise for other people to tell us exactly what our lessons are, as this robs us of our learning. We have to find the answers ourselves while being inspired by those around us, in the same way that I hope you will be inspired by this book, finding your own inner truth, and your own meanings from it.

Example 2
Victimhood

In this example, two mature masculine traits are both good solutions for the immature feminine's victimhood.

The victim is an expression of the immature feminine. It opposes the immature masculine's judgemental nature. Notice if you are judging and comparing yourself to others and how this supports you in being a victim?

To evolve the immature feminine's *victim,* into the mature feminine's expression of *creativity,* we need to embody the trait that opposes it in the mature masculine, which is *wisdom and discernment,* but equally *taking responsibility* is a good fit for most people. The more we can use wisdom and discernment without *judgement* (the immature masculine), the more we can experience creativity. This is about the masculine holding space and giving structure to the feminine. The more of reality that the masculine can encompass, the more of reality the feminine can experience.

To simply say, stop being so judgemental, and then you will not be a victim anymore, or stop being so judgemental and then you will be wise and discerning, is a much harder way of getting to where we want to be. We have to become the mature masculine's expression of wisdom and discernment, to evolve the immature feminine into her creative nature. Likewise, we can't just say: stop being a victim, and then you'll express your mature feminine's creative nature and you will suddenly be able to create the life experiences that you desire. Instead of being a victim to the wants and creations of others, psychology does not work this way for most of us. We must use the duality within ourselves to evolve the polarity.

By stepping into our mature masculine, we become less judgemental and consider more of reality before making decisions. But it is best to do this by being something, not by *not* being something else. It helps to start embodying all our mature masculine traits, so that they support each other, but still with our main focus on what we are working on: in this case, wisdom and discernment.

When we use the Masculine and Feminine Polarity Framework to create change in this way, we can clearly see what we need to do in each quadrant.

- Embody: the opposing mature.
- Evolve: into the mature of that same polarity.
- Avoid: the opposing immature.

By taking the focus away from the immature quadrant that we are experiencing difficulty in, we have a much better chance of evolving from it. So, in relation to our example above, of being a victim in the immature feminine, we need to:

- Embody: responsibility, wisdom and discernment (the mature masculine), and all the other mature masculine traits that fit for us.
- Evolve: into creativity (the mature feminine).
- Avoid: being judgemental (the immature masculine).

And by doing these three things, we indirectly stop being a victim.

Example 3
Shame

Shame, in the immature masculine, opposes the immature feminine's expression of *blaming.* Notice where you feel blame towards yourself, or where you blame others for your feelings.

Where is your feminine blaming you for a situation and where is she blaming others?

To evolve the immature masculine's *shame,* we need to embody the trait that opposes it in the mature feminine, which is *empathy.* The more empathy we have for ourselves, for our depression, and for others, the more we can *honour* someone's point of view and their choices, without taking it personally. Empathy, within ourselves, is about our feminine having empathy for our masculine. The more empathy that our feminine is capable of, the more our masculine can honour himself and honour others.

When we honour who we are, we cannot feel shame. Shame and honouring in one sense are the same energy, so when our focus is on one, the other is not actively experienced. These high *(honouring)* and low *(shameful)* masculine emotional vibrations are of the same energy because, they are two ends of the same pole, like hot and cold are both a temperature, and ice and steam are both expressions of water. When we can recognize our emotions and psychological states in a similar way, *seeing both the polarity and duality of each situation,* thus including the high *(empathy)* and low *(blaming)* feminine vibrational frequencies with the masculine ones: then we understand more of the whole that is making up our experience.

It is through non-resistance and non-attachment that ice and steam will eventually turn back into water, and when working with our emotional states, it is often non-resistance and non-attachment that will serve us the most. Once we embody this knowledge, truly know it and not just understand it, lower vibrational energies don't need to affect us in such negative and resistant ways because our judgement of them is not "bad". We know it is just a temporary expression of energy that also contains the higher vibrational understanding.

At times, this knowledge might even allow us to enjoy lower vibrational energies because we understand the whole, we see more of the truth, and are not trapped in the partial truth of shame. As we realize that judgements keep us trapped in partial truths and it is our vibration that changes our experience of life, which we have control over, then our life starts to change. But even when we have knowledge, and a more complete understanding, we still need to learn how to move through duality, and how to raise our vibration. To simply say stop feeling shameful, and then you will not blame people anymore, is really hard and to just stop blaming people so that we can feel empathy for ourselves and everyone else, is near impossible. Something else needs to happen.

We don't just suddenly stop being an immature person and start being a mature one. It is a process of learning, of self-discovery, and embodying what we learn, mentally and emotionally. We have to work with the mature feminine's nature of empathy to evolve the immature masculine into his honouring nature. When our immature feelings are rooted, expressed, and experienced from the immature masculine, embodying as many of the mature feminine traits as we can, will help not just empathy, but primarily empathy in this example, because that's where our focus is.

Example 4
Arrogance

Next, we will use the immature masculine's expression of *arrogance* as an example. This may look like not valuing or *honouring* the opinions of others, believing that only our point of view matters, whether we verbalize it or not. So, within our own feminine or the feminine of others, we will be encouraging unhealthy *attention-seeking,* self-obsessed, self-absorbed, and selfish behaviours.

The immature masculine's arrogance opposes the immature feminine's attention-seeking behaviour. To evolve the immature masculine's arrogance to his healthy and mature expression of *humbleness,* we need to embody the trait that opposes it in the mature feminine, which is *self-assurance.* To simply say, stop being arrogant, and then you will know humbleness, is unlikely to work. By becoming the mature self-assured feminine, we indirectly evolve the immature masculine from arrogance into humbleness. So, by stepping into our mature feminine, and by being self-assured, we remove the need for arrogance in the masculine, as arrogance in the masculine is the lack of self-assurance in the feminine.

- Embody: the opposing mature.
- Evolve: into the mature of that same polarity.
- Avoid: the opposing immature.

By taking the focus away from the immature quadrant that we are experiencing difficulty in, we have a much better chance of evolving from it.

In relation to our example above, of arrogance in the immature masculine, we:

- Embody: self-assurance (the mature feminine) and all the other mature feminine traits that fit for us.
- Evolve: into humbleness (the mature masculine).
- Avoid: attention-seeking (the immature feminine). By doing this, we indirectly stop being arrogant.

Example 5
Making the Framework Your Own

Some issues that many of us deal with are not on the framework and it's up to us to decide how, and where, we put them. For example: maybe we are *shy* and having problems expressing our self, so we want to be *self-assured*. *Attention-seeking* in the feminine (polarity of self-assurance) does not feel like a good fit, as *humbleness* is not a good solution for our shyness, so we need a different way to get there. *Remember that each person is unique, and there is no one answer for everyone.* Two options are:

1   Anxiousness is similar to shyness in the Feminine and often healed by responsibility and holding space in the masculine, giving us Freedom and Trust in the feminine, which will then dissolve our shyness and give us more self-assurance. This is basically the same method applied in the previous four examples, just without direct correlation on the maps.

2   Alternatively, and more controversially, we can look at how we make humbleness relevant. For real self-assurance in the feminine, we need humbleness in the masculine, but to get there we may need to do shadow work first, and to make our immature healthy.

By consciously developing *arrogance* in our immature masculine: first in an *unhealthy* way; and then in a *healthy* way, as *deserved respect,* we start to give ourselves the information we need to use the polarity framework more effectively. A *healthy immature masculine* makes humbleness more attainable, dissolves our shyness and allows in the feminine self-assurance, that lifts our masculine into humbleness. The advice: *"If you feel shy, then role play at being arrogant",* might seem controversial, but as long as we do this mindfully (not actually *being* condescending or hurting others), we will start to build up the energy that we need in our immature masculine. There is no exact, right way to use the polarity framework as we explore with further examples in chapter Catch 22 and the section, Shadow Work.

It can be really beneficial to sit with the maps and a good friend or partner, simply discussing each other's issues, and how you both best move on the framework, in a light-hearted way. *Maybe the answer today is different to the answer tomorrow: remember that learning through the process is more important than being right about anything or more in one quadrant than another.*

2

Polarity and Duality: What Is the Difference?

What indeed is the difference between polarity and duality? In the dictionary, very little.

From an innate understanding: Polarity is two opposite ends of a spectrum, and duality is the reflection of this spectrum. It is applied in numerous ways and creates the chaos and order that keeps reality spinning. We need both Polarity and Duality in our lives to understand ourselves, and as we understand the interplay between our inner polarity and duality we start to better recognize the dance of creation around us, the dance of masculine and feminine. As we integrate our physical, mental, and emotional bodies, our masculine and feminine; our mature and immature, on every level, in a healthy way, we create such clarity and alignment within ourselves that our "higher self", "soul", "aligned / integrated self" or whatever term works best for us, can work through us. Our intuition, our knowledge, and our power simply become *more* available. The more we recognize the polarity in anything, the more we should also recognize its integration, its oneness, and non-separation; both are always true. The desire for something or the rejection of it is in effect creating the same energy. For example:

- blaming, shaming, empathy, and honouring, all have relations to one another;
- as do attention-seeking, arrogance, self-assurance, and humbleness;
- attachment, ownership, diversity, and interdependence, are all expressions of the same energy on different ends of polarity that is reflected in duality;
- as are anxiousness, avoidance, responsibility, and trust.

The concept of emotional values and traits having both a polarity and duality to them is demonstrated throughout this book.

As we study the four maps, it becomes much clearer that nothing really changes as we move from one quadrant of the framework to another: from anxiousness to trust in the feminine, and from avoidance to responsibility in the masculine, these values are four sides of the same coin. It is our perspective that dictates how we experience different situations from a masculine, feminine, mature, immature, healthy or unhealthy perspective. How we experience a situation entirely depends on our level of consciousness and our vibration at the time. All energy has a vibration and everything we perceive is energy; consciousness is energy, and our emotions are energy. The higher the level of abstraction an energy has, the closer it is to oneness, or wholeness and so the higher the vibration.

A higher vibrational energy which is a higher level of consciousness, simply includes more parts than lower vibrational energies or emotions. This is also paradoxical, because all parts in one sense must include the whole but on an experiential level, the human experience, it is much easier to grasp that our pleasure includes and is made from our pain, than it is the other way around. It is much easier to see that higher vibrational frequencies contain the lower than it is to see the lower ones containing the higher.

This is covered in-depth in the second part of the book, but the general theme is, how do we raise our vibration and expand our consciousness so that we can encompass more of who we are? The deeper we understand and embody the methods presented, which help raise our vibration, the quicker our judgements change. We start to see that most arguments are caused by people looking at the same thing from different angles. Changing our relationship to judgement and our attachment to being right, takes us out of the argument, evolves our awareness, and allows us to see and understand more.

Duality is a gift. Life is a gift. As most of us are not trying to reach enlightenment, transcend separation, suffering and desire, then we need to find a better way to embrace and evolve our dualistic experience. One of the most profound ways to do this is to work with our desire. Many esoteric teachings tell us that we need to transcend all desire to be free, as desire is what keeps us here on earth, in duality. But this often leads to suppression of our unhealthy and lower vibrational desires. Suppression and resistance, are the law of attraction in reverse, so what we resist, we create. We either create it within ourselves or without of ourselves.

Repressing our desires in this way is not helpful, it leads to bigger outbreaks of unhealthy behaviour, crime, and violence, as demonstrated by countries who see a drop in drug and sexually related crimes when they implement more liberal laws, and those who offer restorative justice services, alongside punishment. The real challenge is to transform our desires into healthy ones.

All desires have a healthy and unhealthy expression, so as we create more outlets for our healthy desires, we create a nicer world.

Desire is also connected to our free will, and this is the strongest guiding force when working with polarity and duality, because we always have a choice. The Masculine and Feminine Polarity Framework helps us to see the choices that we have more clearly. It also helps us move to a place of non-judgement, a place where we can look deeper into the gifts that our unhealthy immature and even our shadow brings. It helps us break past conditioning, beliefs and collective dogma.

The cycles between the masculine and feminine, the mature and immature, the healthy and unhealthy, give more depth and complexity to who we are. The cycles create wisdom and give life more meaning and as we go deeper into the model, we start to see that the mature is not always good, and the immature not always bad. By going into and experiencing our unhealthy immature aspects, desires, and sometimes our shadow, we give rise to our greatest growth. As we learn to move beyond the confinements of judgement, becoming able to experience and accept things for how they truly are, we allow ourselves to find liberation and natural alignment, which can look very differently for each of us. The aim of this work is not to make us androgynous, that is, part male and part female, but to recognize and celebrate the differences between masculine and feminine energies, using them as tools to stimulate change and growth.

Three types of change and growth are:

- Devolution (go backwards)
- Revolution (same, but different)
- Evolution (something new)

On the polarity framework, whether we are in a state of evolution or revolution mainly depends on:

- if our situation changes, so we develop a new perspective, our conscious awareness expands, and our understanding deepens (evolution);
- or, if our situation changes, but our perspective largely remains the same, along with our level of conscious, awareness and understanding (revolution).

31

Devolution is not always a bad thing, as long as it's temporary, it simply means that we still have something to learn at this level of consciousness, or that we left the collective behind in our personal development and need to come back and work more for planetary transformation.

Many qualities and traits are not included in the diagrams, such as *hypocritical, humorous, saviour and, rescuer.* Archetypes such as the *warrior, lover, knight, magician, priest, saint, king and queen,* are discussed later.

Once we understand the principles of the framework, it becomes obvious to us which traits belong where, personally for us and for our situation, and which polarity is relevant. The placings on the polarity framework can change at different times for different people; as long as we're not purposefully lying or deceiving ourselves, whatever makes sense for us is best. What remains true throughout, is that to simply stop being something and to start being the opposite of something, its polarity, is much more difficult, than being both the opposing polarity and duality of that something, for example:

It is not easy to move:

- from judgement to discernment;
- from anxious to trusting;
- from attention-seeking to self-assured;
- from the immature masculine to the mature masculine;
- from the immature feminine to the mature feminine.

We are much more likely to move from one immature reaction to another. But to move:

- from attention-seeking to humbleness;
- from judgement to creativity;
- from anxious to responsible;
- from the immature masculine to the mature feminine;
- from the immature feminine to the mature masculine is much easier.

From here, to then work on the duality to increase our mature traits and the relationship between:

- humbleness and self-assurance;
- responsibility and trust;

- creativity and discernment;
- the mature masculine, and the mature feminine and to find the integration of our mature poles, while simultaneously benefiting from their separation, is again, much easier.

We can learn so much about ourselves and integrate much more effectively when we apply both polarity and duality to our situation instead of just polarity. By identifying internal splits and working with this process of polarity and duality, between our masculine and feminine, we actively learn to love ourselves.

The maps give 11 common scenarios, so 44 traits, with love and fear appearing twice, plus another 20 for our shadow. More are suggested and hinted at throughout the book, but keeping flexibility and creativity to the approach is key to getting the most from this work.

The masculine and feminine traits act as a guide only. Traits, emotions and values should not be made binary, as most can be applied with a masculine or feminine energy. Separation in this way is helpful for self-understanding and integration.

At the dawn of Artificial Intelligence (A.I.) we can see that a crude attempt of A.I. could be created by transforming the polarity framework into binary code to facilitate automated emotional depth and maturity, but crude and incomplete it would be. The more we learn of this work the more we see the importance of working multi-dimensionally, of avoiding black and white polarities and instead, focusing on diverse integrations that allows us to maintain mystery. It is within our emotional conflicts and mistakes, as well as our darkness and shadow, that we learn the most about being human and right application of free will.

3
Using the Framework with Others

The dynamics that play out within us are the same dynamics that play out in our partnerships:

- when she manipulates, he becomes controlling.
- he becomes avoidant, so she becomes anxious.
- she blames, he shames.

The four maps work the same within us as they do with another person. As we understand the basic mechanisms behind our reactive behaviour, that our external world is simply a mirror of our internal world, we can move beyond whatever particular story is playing out in our life and look to make the fundamental changes that transform all of the stories in our life. If our partner suddenly starts being a victim: instead of going into our unhealthy masculine, either encouraging or attacking their victim-hood, we can simply take a step back and check ourselves before acting or reacting. *This is a moment in which we might look to the maps for inspiration.* We need to ask ourselves:

"Am I acting from my immature and creating this?"

If yes, we should consider why and which of our needs are not being met. This will prevent us from unconsciously blaming or shaming our partner—becoming anxious, avoidant, or bickering from our immature and shadow expressions. If the answer is *"no, I'm not creating this by acting from my immature"*, then we should gently point out to our partner what we feel is unhealthy about their behaviour, while modelling the associated mature traits from the framework. This stops us instigating negative, defensive reactions in our partner's reply: supporting them to self-analyze and answer maturely.

De-personalizing statements from, *"you are"*, to *"you're being"*, is a subtle but powerful change. As much as we are all individuals with our own masculine and feminine, we are also mirrors for each other. We play multiple opposing masculine and feminine roles for our partners, friends, and colleagues at the same time, thus we need to start consciously helping each other to evolve and mature:

- by realizing the unconscious reactions that come up within us and within our partner(s);
- and by using polarity and duality to mirror what the other needs. Embodying the needed trait(s) from our opposing mature, no matter our or their gender.

There is no set way to mirror and play out duality for someone else, other than we need to display the traits and behaviours that help them to shift back into their Mature. The answer is often changing, so developing our intuition and inner listening skills is always the best way to relate to another.

When we suddenly find ourselves playing the victim, seeking attention, gossiping, or manipulating a situation, we need to use the masculine and feminine framework. Instead of being in our immature feminine and bringing our masculine down, we need to do the opposite. We need to go into our mature masculine and bring our feminine up. We bring her up by addressing what it was in our internal or external world that brought her *(us)* into our immature and into our unhealthy or shadow expressions. This is the basic premise of working with both polarity and duality.

It is very hard to go from an immature feminine trait, to a mature one; from being a victim, to being creative, from one side of the polarity, to the other. It is far easier to move through polarity when we consciously use duality.

Continuing with the example of feminine victimhood, from a few pages ago, this duality could be our inner masculine *(our internal mirror)*, or it might be our partner's or a friend's masculinity *(our external mirror)*. When the feminine is in her victim role, this behaviour can bring our masculine into his immature. Commonly, he will start to judge: to judge the perpetrator himself or her. The act of judging, rightly or wrongly, reinforces victimhood just as acting the victim reinforces judgementalness. What the feminine needs to move from victimhood, are expressions and traits of the mature masculine, for example:

- wisdom and discernment: the polarity of judgement or responsibility, holding space, and boundaries: the polarity of avoidance.

When a person is supported by wisdom and discernment when they take responsibility for their reality, they can no longer be a victim. The inner feminine knows that it is our masculine that makes up our reality in this way. This allows the feminine to move into the opposite of victimhood into creativity. It is almost impossible to be in a victim consciousness while being wise and discerning, they just don't go together, they are not a vibrational match: so victimhood has to turn into creativity, the immature has to turn into the mature when the opposing mature is actively present.

The example above works in correlation as do the four maps and this helps our understanding, but in reality, we are all different. What one person needs to move out of victimhood in a certain situation, might be humbleness or maybe honouring, or selflessness, or any of the other masculine traits. Being in exact correlation is not important. What is important is:

- recognizing the polarity and duality within ourselves and using it to evolve our mature and healthy states of being;
- integrating back into one whole person, knowing that ultimately, we are none of these things and all of them at once.

We need to apply the exact same process when we find ourselves in our immature masculine. We need to go into our mature feminine, and ask:

- what am I resisting?
- what am I pushing away?
- what is it about myself that I am not willing to accept?

And then we need to learn to fully love and accept this part of ourselves, however long that may take. We need to accept our pain and our dark side, that part of us that we feel is unacceptable. It is the parts of us that we do not accept, that push us into fear and our immature expressions. It is only from this acceptance, that real transformation and change can occur.

To evolve our masculine, we must use the mature feminine traits and be empathic, accepting, demonstrate self-assurance, and use our intuition. We must find a way to feel safe enough to trust.

And to evolve the feminine, we must use the mature masculine traits and be humble and wise, have emotional and mental balance, strength, bravery, and mindfulness. We must be able to honour all life.

Through judging less and raising our vibration, our perspectives change much quicker from the immature to the mature. In the same way, if we are suddenly being overly competitive or judgemental and possessive, then we need to look to our inner feminine to see what we are not fully accepting. To see what moved us into unhealthy fear-based expressions thus leaving a lack in our healthy expressions of the immature masculine. And on the unconscious level, *'why'* did we allow it? When we can witness the immature within ourselves and simply accept it, it does not need to last for long, it is our resistance to our immature that perpetuates more unhealthy, immature behaviour. We are all constantly going through this most basic cycle of growth, the cycle of chaos and order. This cycle deepens our knowledge, our knowing, and our understanding each time. Finding gratitude for our immature and even our shadow, helps us grow and embody a non-judgemental attitude.

Instead of "non-judgementalness" being a concept that we apply, it becomes a natural response. It becomes our natural response because we are developing the ability to be grateful; grateful for all our traits and aspects: mature, immature, healthy, unhealthy, and our shadow. The dynamic that plays out within us is the same dynamic that plays out in our relationships. Therefore, it is important to first and foremost develop the relationship we have with ourselves. If we start using the polarity framework with others before we are ready, before we have successfully used it on our own big issues, we run the risk of pushing the other into their victim, their immature feminine.

We become the rescuer from our immature masculine, unconsciously proving our own self-worth to ourselves, dominating the situation and demonstrating our intellect with arrogance. No matter how pure our intention and desire to genuinely help is, we will still create a dynamic of making them the victim or some other twisted interaction and unhealthy expression of our masculine and feminine traits. When we can move into our own mature feminine to evolve our own immature masculine and our own mature masculine to evolve our own immature feminine, then we are ready to do this with and for others.

4
Intention and Purpose

The purpose of life changes depending on what we need to learn; different people will feel and express purpose differently, some examples include:

- the purpose of life is to enjoy life;
- the purpose of life is for our soul to learn lessons;
- the purpose of life is to transform fear into love;
- the purpose of life is to serve God;
- life has no purpose; the purpose is to make it our own;
- the purpose of life is . . .

It does not matter so much what we feel our purpose is, but to work with logic from our healthy immature masculine, we need a purpose, an aim, a plan, or a strategy, the immature masculine loves these things. Having a purpose or mission in life is useful to help us transform, it gives us something to refer back to when we feel we are going in the wrong direction. Bear in mind, that we can have more than one purpose and change it any time we wish, *so it is really good to write something down for this next exercise and before moving on with the book.*

Specific Intentions

Having an intention related to a specific issue or theme in our life is a really helpful tool. Using the masculine and feminine polarity maps with the two processes below, is a great way to help us find such specific issues.

Exploration Exercise

1 Using the maps, pick one immature trait that you identify with.
2 Write down how you experience this immature trait and how it affects you and your life. Remember: immature does not always mean unhealthy, negative, or bad.
3 Now find the opposing mature trait. For example, if you picked, "attention-seeking" in the feminine as your immature trait, then

the opposing mature trait would be "humbleness" in the masculine. Write down how this mature trait plays out in your life. It can be good to ask:

- how did, or didn't, my parents and role models demonstrate this trait when I was growing up?
- how do I experience it in my culture, within my social circle, my workplace, and the country I live in?
- how do I define it? *Often our personal meanings differ, and some people experience mature traits in an unhealthy way*
- how does this trait play out in my close intimate relationships with my life partner and friends?

4 Write down ways you can embody this mature trait to evolve the immature trait that you picked in step one, e.g.: how can embodying humbleness help you to stop seeking attention and to be more self-assured?

Intention Exercise

1 From the previous exercise, looking at how you can embody a mature trait to help you evolve an immature trait:

- write down what you need to release, what you need to let go of, and what is stopping you;
- now write down how your life will be different once you have released whatever is holding you back:
  – *what will life be like without the pain?*
  – *what will life be like when I embody this mature trait?*

2 Create your intention and positive affirmation. It should be positive: how you want to feel and how you want life to be. Not what you want to release. Your intention should be similar to the positive answers from the last questions. Here are a couple of examples:

"I love and accept myself."

"I am confident and self-assured. I walk into every situation with ease and grace."

Your personal intention is the new vibration that you are going to attract into your life. When working with polarity and duality, positive affirmations, hypnosis, neuro-linguistic programming (NLP), and other methods that work with the mind through repetition are important, but only half the solution. The other half of the solution is finding ways to be authentic with ourselves, creating physical, mental, and emotional alignment, while ensuring that we are being authentic and honest with ourselves when pain is there, but not allowing it to dominate our thoughts and intentions.

5
Self-Love and Acceptance

It is our mature feminine that can love and accept us completely. All the parts of our lives, all the things that we judge as bad, what we are ashamed of, or wish we could change. Our mature feminine can love all these parts of our life, in the same way that we would hope a mother would love a newborn child. The feminine knows that our pain and suffering can lead to our greatest gifts, so it is easier for her not to judge. Our masculine *cannot* love and accept unconditionally. The immature masculine is judgemental, and the mature masculine is wise and discerning. He is there to make sure that we take the correct actions to build a healthy ego and sense of separate self, an ego that creates joy, beauty, and happiness. He simply cannot accept all our pain and suffering, the masculine is here to change the world, not accept it. Ultimately, the masculine loves, and accepts us completely, because he is integrated with the feminine, but to be a whole and complete person, we need both parts:

We need to love and accept ourselves completely and *change things within ourselves.*

The importance of, and a path to self-love is discussed more in the Physical, Mental, and Emotional Bodies section of this book.

6
Always Four People in Any Relationship

There are never two people in a relationship, there are always four: your inner masculine and feminine, and their inner masculine and feminine. Society and mainstream media often teach us that we are incomplete, that as a feminine heterosexual woman, we need to find a masculine heterosexual man, aka, *our other half,* or the other way around, if we are a man. We come together to make one whole person. In these kinds of relationships, we unconsciously sacrifice a part of ourselves and one of our greatest opportunities for growth and self-development. We need to acknowledge that we already are a whole person and when we find someone who we want to be with, we come together as two complete people to make a greater whole.

For most people, we are attracted to our opposite, someone who is similar to and matches our inner masculine or feminine:

- so, a masculine man will be attracted to a feminine woman, who feels like his own inner feminine;
- and a feminine woman will be attracted to a masculine man, who feels like her own inner masculine.

This dynamic changes for each of us to fit our own complex makeup of masculine and feminine polarities. It's best to create a healthy relationship within ourselves before investing too heavily in relationships without. Put very simply, reality is a mirror, that mirrors back to us who we are. We live in a vibrational universe governed by the law of attraction; this should have been proven to each of us over and over again throughout life. If not, try to look a little deeper and observe how thoughts and actions match reality. As we change our thoughts, beliefs, and behaviours, and as we evolve our inner masculine and feminine, our reality changes with us.

As we practise this universal truth, we come to know that the deeper and more loving relationship we have between our inner masculine and feminine, the deeper and more loving relationships we will attract. And as we evolve all of our traits and expressions to be healthy, we will attract someone who is a healthy opposite to us. Someone who opposes us in all the right ways, but loves themselves, and so can love us too.

The law of attraction is always working with the law of polarity. Due to the uniqueness and complexities of individual personalities, there are no fixed rules:

- sometimes opposites attract and sometimes they repel;
- sometimes similarities attract and sometimes they repel;
- often, we will repel and attract at the same time, and how polarity plays out will depend on what we need to learn and integrate.

As we consciously use our free will to work with these laws, we create more desirable experiences and better vibrational matches.

In Relation to Partnerships

Although each of us is a whole and independent person and all relationships and partnerships in life become better once we can demonstrate this, our consciousness is always connecting, learning, and evolving, with our partner's, creating vibrational matches where we integrate together more, and creating separation and polarization where we do not. This, in turn, creates new opportunities for integration that expands and deepens our personality and consciousness as a whole.

Example 1

When we do not fully love and accept ourselves, we are likely to attract a partner whose non-predominant side does not fully love and accept us either. This is one of the ways that our partner, or partners, act as mirrors for us.

So, if we are a masculine man, and don't fully love and accept ourselves, then a common relationship dynamic is that when the woman we are in a relationship with goes into her immature masculine, we will find it hard to love and accept her. We are looking at what we don't like about ourselves *(or our former self if we've done a lot of self-development work)*. We're trying to love the parts of us that we judge as unlovable. But as we find her behaviour *(which is normally a lot of our behaviour)*, as unacceptable and to a point unlovable, both of us end up in our masculine. When we're both in our masculine, it's much more likely that power struggles emerge. Everything that's in us, that we do not like can, and generally will, be mirrored back to us by our partner's immature masculine and feminine.

Vicious Circle 1

Our partner mirrors the part of us that we do not like or love, and thus, this is imprinted into us further. So, we become more of what we do not like, reinforcing the original behaviours that we wanted to change in the first place.

Vicious Circle 2

And because our partner is mirroring the part of us that we don't like or love in that moment, we are unable to love them, their new imprint is also of not being lovable.

To turn a vicious circle into a virtuous one, we must use our free will, this means both parties choosing to act from their healthy mature. When mirroring back our partner's inner masculine or feminine, we need to give them the imprint of our unique mature masculine or feminine, mixed with the best of other individuals who have influenced our life. This is how we evolve, together. We mirror back the best of our partner's masculine or feminine, everything we love and appreciate about them, with what we are grateful for and at the same time we add something new—we add our highest to help evolve their best.

Example 2

If we love and accept ourselves fully, but our partner does not, somewhere they are not loving themselves enough, they are not a complete vibrational match for our self-love. If their unhealthy ego starts to polarize the situation, then the more they love us, the less they may start to love themselves.

Example 3

Similarly, if we feel that someone broke our heart, then it is very likely that polarity is working without a method of integration. The vibrational match between two hearts changed and created polarization. The more one loves, the less the other can. Thus, the more the person who feels their heart is broken loves, the more it hurts, often in an addictive self-destructive way.

Owning Our Inner Selves

In the paradigm where our partner is literally our other half, we can fail to develop our inner masculine or feminine, as we have not been taught to recognize it for what it truly is. We may find ourselves feeling like we are turning into our partner. Different people will deal with this differently, depending on their beliefs. The general theme, in this paradigm, is that people don't take responsibility for their own inner masculine and feminine. When we don't take responsibility for ourselves and acknowledge our inner masculine and feminine that is similar to our partner—thus, why we are attracted to them and are heavily influenced by them—we are projecting, projecting our love and our fears, focusing on the masculine and feminine without but not within.

Another downside of not owning and acknowledging our inner masculine and feminine, is that there can be a lack of diversity in the relationship. For couples without family, many friends, or colleagues, there is a particular danger that they are not owning and developing their uniqueness. They are becoming less, both individually, and as a couple. You can see when couples lose their individuality, because they start to finish each other's sentences too often, and often have long periods of silence between themselves.

There is nothing wrong with lots of silence in a relationship: for the mature masculine it can be blissful, but this couple needs more polarity, more creative conflict, more tension, and more great sex. The tensions should be happy and joyful, enabling them to be more of themselves, each bringing more of their unique expression that supports the other to express more of their unique expressions in turn. The differences between our masculinity and femininity should complement and increase each other. When we can no longer distinguish polarity: then we are either very highly evolved, constantly expressing our pure, integrated, and higher self, or we have a problem.

The false belief that we are not already whole and "need" another to be so, is held by so many people and societies around the world, that it can sometimes be hard to get away from. It is like a constant unspoken cultural belief being propagated out of ignorance. Applying the tools and principles in this book helps us to transcend judgement:

- to understand and change our childhood conditioning;
- to love and accept ourselves more;
- and to know that we are all already whole and complete people.

From here it is so much easier to find a partner who matches us if we wish someone we can grow and learn with.

7

Happy Immature Lives and Being Single

⌒

Many couples can live relatively happy and successful lives while acting mostly from their immature. A man can be very masculine, dominant, competitive and thrive in a capitalist environment. This type of personality can put his partner completely into her feminine, and she can feel so much freedom while being perfectly happy to gossip about other people, be the centre of attention, while spending her time manipulating him and making him feel jealous to increase his attraction to her. Indeed, for many people this is a sign of a successful relationship: money, power, a deep bond, and the envy of their peers.

Acting from our immature does not necessarily make us *bad* people, but more often than not, it is keeping us locked in separation. From here, we can live our lives from our unhealthy ego in an almost constant state of reaction. Most behavioural changes we experience will come from the reinforcement and development of our ego into further separation. There may be moments of wisdom and insight from our mature masculine and moments of unselfish accepting love from our mature feminine that allow us a break from our unconscious reactions, but ultimately, we need to evolve.

Most people's immature is based in the unhealthy ego and although moments of separation can be great for our growth and we can be happy in them, getting lost in them stops our growth and evolution.

It is often harder to live a happy and immature life when single. When we are single, we don't have such a good mirror to reinforce our immature behaviour with positivity, praise, rewarding experiences, and the chemicals in the brain that support them. When we are single, it can be hard to find someone who is the right fit for all of our immature and mostly unhealthy behaviours. Circles of friends can do this to a degree, but more often than not, somewhere our or their immature behaviour is experienced as negative and that deep bond and feeling of satisfaction is not there. When we are acting from our mature, it's easy for other people to be a good mirror for us, as positivity from the mature does not need a specific "type of person" to mirror it back in a healthy and positive way. However, we still fit better with some people, more than we do with others.

When we are in an intimate relationship with another, even when apart, their energy is with us. So, although our masculine and feminine are completely unique to us, we are evolving with them, it is growing, and it is finding space through our relationship with them. This happens with our friends and family too and sometimes, even our colleagues. But when we have an intimate or sexual relationship with someone, it increases. It is really important to remember that although we are whole and complete people, and our inner masculine and feminine are ours alone, in our close relationships our inner masculine and feminine can really feel like our partner is inside of us and from one perspective they are, because we take an imprint of them into ourselves.

They mirror us and we grow through them, but our main focus should always be on ourselves, our inner masculine and feminine. When we learn to work with their imprint inside of us, it becomes easier to learn how to love and accept ourselves and then in turn, we can truly love them. Some of us may try and can benefit from learning the lessons that being single teaches us without necessarily leaving our relationship: undoing co-dependency issues that have built up over the years through the integration of unhealthy immature and shadow aspects.

Being Single

When the mind is purposefully deciding to be single, to focus on self-development, in order to attract a "better" partner, a better reflection of ourselves that we find "easy" to love but our physical body wants sex now and our emotional body wants love now, alignment can seem impossible. But by allowing our three bodies to communicate with each other, letting our heart know that we are choosing to become a better version of ourselves, thus sacrificing what our heart wants in the moment so it can have alignment in the future; then the heart can express sadness to move back to joy, but not fully, *as to the heart being happy and fulfilled in the here and now is all there is. To the heart, time does not exist and there is only NOW, the time is always now, thus it's very important to learn to love ourselves* if we are to find alignment, if we are to have a happy heart.

Our physical body (our sex), can then start to consciously cultivate the sexual energy needed to attract our aligned partner of the future; this level of communication between our three bodies allows inner understanding, if *not* inner alignment. Communication between our three bodies may not work as well in relation to *"marrying for money"* or *"staying together for the children"* so in cases like these, it's important to find ways to meet desires in each of our three bodies while being as conscious as we can about why we are making the sacrifices that we are making. *Not having alignment in our three bodies means not having access to our full power.*

The self-acceptance and self-love movement is an amazing and needed paradigm shift that is happening in the world, but it really is okay to decide *not* to accept something about ourselves and to change it instead. Our masculine does not accept everything in the world, it's our feminine that loves and accepts everything and this balance is essential for healthy integration and a healthy life. It's much better if we don't drop into self-hate and loathing when we decide we don't like something about ourselves, but if we do, we should accept that this is the human paradox and avoid hating ourselves for hating ourselves as we wait for things to change, thus choosing to be single until we are able to attract a partner that we are *happier* with.

On an individual level, we may simply say: "I go to the gym and I look after my body and improve myself, because I love myself."

During times in our life when we actually are single or celibate, we may start to notice the desires of our non-predominant traits. We might find ourselves having sexual desires polarized from how we normally feel, because our inner masculine or feminine does not have an outlet through our partner, thus, our subconscious thoughts and desires start to become more conscious and we start to recognize conflicting polarities within ourselves. Being single can also create misalignment between our physical, mental, and emotional bodies, as it's difficult to follow conflicting desires.

In these cases managing our sexual and emotional desires is not always easy. Working with sexual desire is a lifelong learning for most, if not all of us, no matter if married or single because with it we can generate energy. Sexual energy, coupled with fantasy can support us to evolve: the key is to focus on the energy more than the mental fantasy, but still using the mental fantasy and polarity to help evolve our psychology and increase our energy. The energy is our prime concern because this magnifies our use of the law of attraction, thus, our ability to attract in life what we focus on.

When single (or if in a relationship using our imagination and past experience), it can be helpful to ask ourselves:

- When and how do our sexual desires and yearnings manifest and more importantly, when and how do they manifest in polarization to what we consciously want?

Sometimes, these fantasies may feel perverted or about domination, submission, homosexuality or lesbianism, so we do not allow ourselves to really experience or even acknowledge that they are there, but when we understand them as *repressed and unhealthy immature desires from our inner masculine or feminine, because we do not have a partner to project them into,* they become easier to accept.

Even if we are a feminine woman wanting to attract a relationship with a feminine woman, the level of and type of masculine energy in us, will dictate the partner that we attract and the type of masculine energy within them, so it's important to cultivate it in the way we want to receive it back.

When working with sexual desire and fantasy in general, if there is an authentic rejection *not* from guilt or shame for homosexual or similar desires, but an authentic rejection and feeling that *"this is wrong", "this is not me", "not what I want",* then we might need to see where our three bodies, our *heart,* our *sex,* and our *mind,* are not in alignment because this means that the energy we are rejecting is still being cultivated inside of us. Thus, this is the energy that we use to attract our future partner *so, we attract someone who matches our unhealthy immature desires* instead of our healthy ones.

Using Sexual Polarity

Once we understand emotional and sexual polarity—in that often, *our repressed sexual desires are the desires designed to be imprinted into our partner* which they transform, evolve, and put back into us—we can begin to accept *all* sexual aspects of our self more easily if we did not already.

In drawing inspiration from sexual energy and fantasy, it's helpful to remember that developing a healthy sexual loving relationship with our self, *our masculine and feminine,* is one of the best things that we can do for a happy life and to attract a partner because, we are cultivating our own sexual energy and the fantasies that are in alignment with our higher self. But when we have a lot of unexpressed, repressed, and subconscious sexual desires, these are more likely to become immature, creating unhealthy fantasies such as those connected to the world of BDSM, domination, and submission. How these translate is unique for each of us, but if we have fantasies about whips, chains, slavery, and bondage, try to remember that to attract the partner of our dreams, we need to maintain our sovereignty and find the healthy desires within our dark shadow fantasies so we should work to understand and transform these as discussed in the section "Shadow Work".

Understanding and imprinting the healthier aspects of our dark shadow fantasies into our inner masculine or feminine will support us in attracting our perfect partner, because this is one of the gifts that we have for them: the full spectrum of our sexuality, including our shadow, but healed conscious and mature; whether this still contains aspects of BDSM or not is completely our choice, but it's always wise to identify the spiritual impulses behind any kinks as by understanding these, we understand ourselves, our uniqueness, and more.

Sexual shadow desires and fantasies can be very powerful when we know how to use them. What is important is to not be consumed by them when on a journey of self-understanding and shadow work. If we have been single for a long time, or been hurt through loneliness, we might have gone too far into our shadow with abusive fantasies, sexual and non-sexual, towards ourselves and others. How our personal shadows manifest can be different for each of us depending on many factors including psychology, but applying an abstract perspective and seeing how our internal masculine and feminine dynamics created the shadow can really help us to move out of it and learn what it is trying to teach us. Working with our shadow in general terms is covered later.

Things are rarely straightforward when looking at sexual fantasy with polarity, and we may have to explore our inner self using polarity and duality many times to find our truth, as momentary as our truth may be.

Open Relationships

People living more from their mature masculine and feminine are more likely to choose to be single, celibate, or to have developed "successful" open or polyamorous relationships than those who are not. But for many of these people, polyamorous relationships may not be the right choice. These relationships can create a lot of immature masculine and feminine scenarios, which can be great for long-term development and growth, but if we are not willing or do not have the time to do the inner work, then the results can be disastrous. In my personal opinion, you need a community, physical or online, practising open relationships who have gone through a cultural change related to issues of attachment, jealousy, and ownership when embarking on this journey.

People who are only practising emotional polyamory, deep platonic love relations with many and only one sexual partner or people who have a committed relationship with one person but sexual relationships outside without emotional intimacy, have a greater chance of success in open relationships. But to have both sex and emotional intimacy with multiple people can be very challenging from the perspective of our inner masculine and feminine.

8

Why Women (the Mature Feminine) Seem to Be Evolving More Quickly

~

While our immature can be both healthy and unhealthy, it's normally easier for women to create a relatively healthy immature masculine, because there is less collective dogma and expectations connected to their immature masculine through their gender. Men are likely to have more unhealthy behaviours in their immature masculine from childhood and societal conditioning, because the immature masculine governs most of our society, with men traditionally being responsible for tasks connected to the immature masculine.

Generally, it is easier for all of us to step into our mature feminine, than it is our mature masculine, because of several common reasons:

- When a child is born, regardless of sex, the mature feminine traits come before the masculine, mothering comes before fathering.
- In relation to our own healing, the mature feminine is acceptance and it's through loving and accepting ourselves that our old pain and trauma can transform.
- When we have a lot of pain and trauma, the masculine can almost be paralyzed until our mature feminine can start accepting and loving our whole self. So generally, the feminine becomes mature first, allowing us to accept a situation before taking action.
- True healing and transformation happens through acceptance; without it we cannot heal. Where the immature masculine judges, the mature masculine applies discernment, wisdom, and knowing. He chooses the correct action and takes it. As vital as our mature masculine is, he cannot unconditionally accept our pain and trauma to transform it, this is our feminine's role.

In society and the collective structures that govern us, the mature feminine is reflected much more than the mature masculine, with the immature masculine being the most predominant. The mature masculine threatens many ways of thinking that keep society operating the way that it does. The mature feminine, expressing herself through motherhood, is much more widely accepted and encouraged in almost every area of society: to be caring, creative, artistic, self-assured, and confident is encouraged. The mature masculine's expression of fatherhood can be spotted in some religious, new age and progressive culture contexts, while sports, politics, history, bars and night clubs, TV, film, and media, are all dominated by the immature masculine: the immature unhealthy father and the masculine shadow. The immature masculine is our model for society and it encompasses many global issues: ownership and slavery; imprisonment, violence, prejudice, and racism; rule of intellect; competitiveness; warmongering; dictation.

Looking at interdependence, co-operation, humbleness, selflessness, worship, and responsibility, we can see that many of us have been conditioned to view mature masculine traits negatively. So how do we change an immature masculine world, into a balanced, integrated, healthy, mature one? On the collective scale, the feminine needs to be mature to help the immature masculine evolve. This means *each man and woman needs to develop their feminine to listen to their intuition and to trust. To forgive the past and to heal trauma through acceptance* that is eventually aiming for unconditional self-love and compassion. Countries need to forgive each other as do cities and towns, the north, south, east, west divides of a community. Collective values of racism, religious righteousness, and other prejudices in certain groups of people need to transform out of the masculine shadow.

If it feels that some aspects of the world are becoming overly soft and feminine, while others are turning into a living hell, then we would be wise to look at both the polarity and duality of the situation. To see how the discrepancies we experience in the wider world are mirrored into our own lives. We must look into ourselves and ask, *"Is our feminine only being mature when a situation is nice, pleasant, and safe?"* and if the answer is *"yes"*, then *"Is our feminine moving into the immature, reacting from fear, and what we do not want to experience, thus creating it elsewhere in the world?"*

From a non-dual perspective, sentences like *"it's not me, it's them"*, make little sense because life is a mirror and everything is connected; all that makes sense is to find what is not in alignment within ourselves and then use the polarity of our masculine and feminine energies to heal it.

The above question can be very hard to ask ourselves and the answer *"yes"*, is one of the main reasons why the mature masculine is so lacking in our world today. So, to repeat the question: *"Is our feminine only being mature when a situation is nice, pleasant, and safe?"*

Evolving the Masculine and Feminine

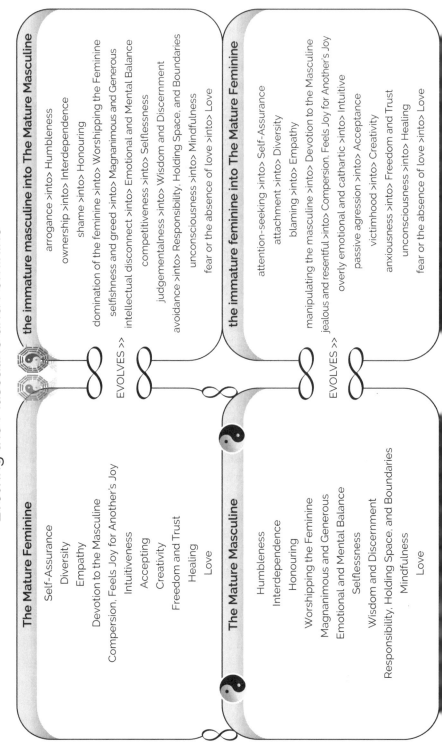

The Mature Feminine

Self-Assurance

Diversity

Empathy

Devotion to the Masculine

Compersion. Feels Joy for Another's Joy

Intuitiveness

Accepting

Creativity

Freedom and Trust

Healing

Love

the immature masculine into The Mature Masculine

arrogance >into> Humbleness

ownership >into> Interdependence

shame >into> Honouring

domination of the feminine >into> Worshipping the Feminine

selfishness and greed >into> Magnanimous and Generous

intellectual disconnect >into> Emotional and Mental Balance

competitiveness >into> Selflessness

judgementalness >into> Wisdom and Discernment

avoidance >into> Responsibility, Holding Space, and Boundaries

unconsciousness >into> Mindfulness

fear or the absence of love >into> Love

EVOLVES >>

The Mature Masculine

Humbleness

Interdependence

Honouring

Worshipping the Feminine

Magnanimous and Generous

Emotional and Mental Balance

Selflessness

Wisdom and Discernment

Responsibility, Holding Space, and Boundaries

Mindfulness

Love

the immature feminine into The Mature Feminine

attention-seeking >into> Self-Assurance

attachment >into> Diversity

blaming >into> Empathy

manipulating the masculine >into> Devotion to the Masculine

jealous and resentful >into> Compersion. Feels Joy for Another's Joy

overly emotional and cathartic >into> Intuitive

passive agression >into> Acceptance

victimhood >into> Creativity

anxiousness >into> Freedom and Trust

unconsciousness >into> Healing

fear or the absence of love >into> Love

EVOLVES >>

Devolving the Masculine and Feminine

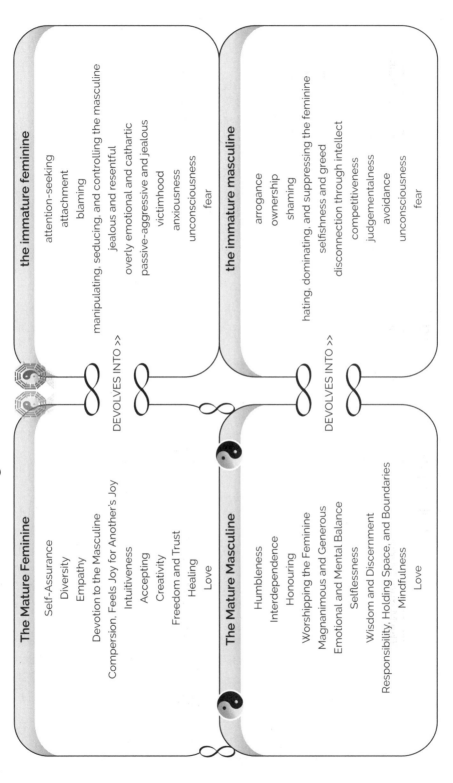

The Mature Feminine

Self-Assurance
Diversity
Empathy
Devotion to the Masculine
Compersion, Feels Joy for Another's Joy
Intuitiveness
Accepting
Creativity
Freedom and Trust
Healing
Love

DEVOLVES INTO >>

the immature feminine

attention-seeking
attachment
blaming
manipulating, seducing, and controlling the masculine
jealous and resentful
overly emotional and cathartic
passive-aggressive and jealous
victimhood
anxiousness
unconsciousness
fear

The Mature Masculine

Humbleness
Interdependence
Honouring
Worshipping the Feminine
Magnanimous and Generous
Emotional and Mental Balance
Selflessness
Wisdom and Discernment
Responsibility, Holding Space, and Boundaries
Mindfulness
Love

DEVOLVES INTO >>

the immature masculine

arrogance
ownership
shaming
hating, dominating, and suppressing the feminine
selfishness and greed
disconnection through intellect
competitiveness
judgementalness
avoidance
unconsciousness
fear

9
The Unhealthy Mature

Sometimes we act with traits associated with our mature self, but in fact, we are being unhealthy and damaging ourselves. For example, humbleness in the mature masculine can be expressed in a very unhealthy way. Perhaps we are constantly playing small, not living our full potential, and not helping to build a new and beautiful world because we want to be humble. Doing this is a disservice to ourselves and the world, to be humble should not mean to sacrifice ourselves and not to do our best. To be authentically humble, can only happen when we have actually done our best.

Our best can come from selflessness, but rarely sacrifice. The mature masculine cannot back down and let the immature masculine collect all of the money, fame, and power because he wants to be humble. This is not humble, it is weak, and the mature masculine is anything but weak. Conserving our energy and not entering into verbal fights, as they are a tool for manipulation that can pull us into our immature, is very different to being weak. But even in these cases, the mature masculine must be looking to take action that helps the immature and the whole evolve.

The mature masculine does not need to fight in the traditional sense, but he does need to win, and the only winning scenario for the mature masculine is a win-win.

In this scenario of unhealthy mature humbleness, there is also the risk of his feminine moving into her immature Shadow, because when the masculine is being overly "humble", the immature feminine may have the desire to "seek attention", but if the masculine stays in his mature expression, her unexpressed need for attention turns into her shadow of self-harming (shadow polarities are discussed later).

It can be really helpful to read this next section with a printed copy of the mirror map.

The two examples below show how our mature traits can become unhealthy and how this often creates shadow aspects within ourselves. It is about as complex as it gets, so do read it twice if you don't follow. And don't forget that both of these examples are happening inside one person, which for this example is a man.

1 The immature feminine's "attention-seeking", opposes "humbleness" in
the mature masculine. So, if our feminine sees unhealthy humbleness
in the masculine, she will try to move the masculine into his immature
behaviour of arrogance. This could be seen as a good thing, as she
wants to protect him from what unhealthy humbleness brings.
She wants him to take what he earns and accept the credit, praise,
and power that his actions create; she wants the masculine to learn
deserved respect, which is transforming arrogance into its healthy
expression as she feels he is not ready for humbleness, but if she fails
to move him into the immature expressions that would take him out
of humbleness, it means that she is likely to move into her opposing
feminine shadow, of self-harming, to create balance.

2 Another expression of the unhealthy mature masculine can happen
through selflessness. This entails giving so much of ourselves away due
to our own high expectations, that overall, we become less and have less
to give to the world. The masculine has outgrown his unhealthy and
immature expressions of competitiveness, but he has not fully learnt
to protect himself. This could be his finances, his energy, or his body,
if he allows his physique to deteriorate: this can cause the shadow of
the immature feminine to take over. The immature feminine's passive-
aggressiveness opposes selflessness in the mature masculine, or whichever
immature trait feels like the right fit for you, so she tries to bring the
masculine back into his immature competitive nature. This could
be seen as a good thing, as she wants to protect him from unhealthy
selflessness. She wants him to delve deeper into lessons of the immature,
while also being able to fight and compete for what he needs. He might
go into unhealthy competitiveness, or he could go into a healthy version
of competitiveness, working in a team, and always making his enemy
stronger, although for the mature masculine, there are no real enemies,
just states of being that require him to act in a certain way.

He would normally never want to leave anyone in a weaker position than
when they started while he grows stronger, as doing this goes against the
mature masculine's nature and only means that the challenges that he can
face in later life have been reduced, so ultimately his potential for development and evolution have been reduced. From the feminine's perspective,
she feels that he is not ready for selflessness and has greater lessons to learn

through competition, healthy competition, the healthy immature. If she fails to move him into his immature, to learn these lessons, then she is likely to move into her opposing shadow of *hatred and spite,* because he, the man, is unable to experience the passive-aggressive tendencies that his unhealthy selflessness created. So now, a part of the feminine acts from the immature shadow of resentment, hatred, and spite, while the mature masculine demonstrates unhealthy selflessness.

This can be in the conscious or the subconscious mind and it will remain this way until something changes in the man's life or until he acknowledges and chooses to change it.

Taking It Personally

If we take something personally, then in general one of two things are happening:

1 The person we are communicating with is in their own drama, in their immature, completely disconnected from us and the collective consciousness. If in that moment, instead of recognizing and accepting this, we also act from our immature, by taking their behaviour personally, then we create drama. We create drama around something that is fundamentally false and that we should never have taken personally in the first place.

2 The action that we are feeling attacked by, are taking personally, is repressed somewhere within us. By acknowledging this and working to transform it within ourselves, we are indirectly transforming it within them and within the collective consciousness, so we don't need to attract it anymore. This is often as simple:
   – as recognizing the other as our mirror;
   – and then taking responsibility for how we feel and act, regardless of what they said, did, or did not say or do.

When we take something personally, we "react". When we take responsibility, we "act from mindfulness".

In the second scenario, when we have taken something personally that's not a compliment or appreciation, as these are best to accept with gratitude and without attachment, then we are probably acting from our immature.

Our immature masculine traits of:

- arrogance (everything is about me);
- ownership (they stole from me);
- shame (shaming ourselves or needing to shame others in retaliation);
- judgementalness (judging, and comparing our standpoint, to others).

Or our immature feminine traits of:

- attention-seeking (by taking it personally, drama, and excitement is created even if negative);
- attachment (their view jeopardizes my position and what I hold dear);
- blaming (blaming others or blaming ourselves);
- victimhood (feeling attacked by their point of view).

In all of these situations, our immature has something to learn, somewhere to grow, or something to deepen within our personality. We need to not beat ourselves up about it, knowing that when we can observe ourselves taking something personally, we are already halfway to not taking it personally. As always, if we feel stuck, then it's good to take out the polarity framework maps to see how the polarity and duality is in our situation, what lessons can be learned, and what wants to change within us.

War, Peace, and Freedom

When setting an intention, it's good to be aware that intentions of peace and freedom, while beautiful, are not always helpful. When peace and freedom are our intention, we are generally more focused on escaping what we do not want, without *explicitly admitting what the problem is.* The subconscious is locked and focused on what it is trying to escape.

As human beings at this point of evolution, when we have peace, but don't know what we want to do with our peace, we will generally start wars and arguments to help us realize what we do want.

War and peace are simply polarities, with war giving us the resistance needed to understand ourselves. As violence lowers our vibration and stops our evolution, it's important to reframe and understand our need for war, fights, and arguments as our need for resistance; we can then start to harness the benefits from the conflicts that we have with ourselves and with others.

As we expand our awareness, we no longer need to fight with enemies, but instead, can work with friends in a way that gives the resistance needed for us all to develop, grow, and be strong. The more resistant and resilient our friends are, the more resistant and resilient we are. The key is learning to channel this war-like energy in a constructive, conscious, and loving way, even if it hurts and destroys things in the process. To try taking the concept of war away from humanity is pointless, but to see the natural polarity of war in relation to our desire for peace, means we can create a healthy and non-violent relationship to the concept of war. From a meta perspective of duality, we need fear in our life so that we can understand love and we need war, or resistance in life, so that we can realize what we want, meaning we become ready for peace.

Similarly, if we have freedom but we are not living our full potential or have no meaningful purpose in life, then the best we can wish for is someone we respect and trust who has our best interests at heart, who will listen to our feedback, *to restrict us and tell us no.* It's the restrictions to our freedom that often allow us to find out what we want: the moment someone takes something away from us, we realize what we had and what we want—we create an aim, purpose, passion and decide what is worth fighting for. The lyrics of a Joni Mitchell song: *"you don't know what you've got till it's gone"* expresses the truth of it.

Of course, life is better when we know the real value of everything that we have, but some people need to lose something in order to understand it's worth and then fight for it again to really appreciate it. For these reasons, I strongly suggest when setting an intention, avoid *"I want peace",* or *"I want freedom",* as on the soul and spiritual level, we have these things already and can experience them momentarily, through meditation and spiritual practice, but as to being here, alive, and living in duality, focus on the questions:

"What will I do when I have peace, what do I want to feel other than peace?"
and
"What will I do when I have freedom, what do I want my freedom for?"

Thereby appreciating and being grateful for all that we have, we will create less war in our lives and less restrictions, and when war, arguments, and conflicts arise, we don't need to be afraid, but to see all opponents as friends, teaching us lessons, seeing each act of conflict as an act of *tough love* that makes all parties stronger. All men are brothers and all women are sisters.

10
Making the Immature Healthy
~~

A dynamic of cultural evolution, as described by Dr Clare Graves and Don Beck in "Spiral Dynamics", shows how we collectively and continuously move through the cycle of, *express self, sacrifice self, express self, sacrifice self.* From, *"I"*, to *"We"*, to *"I"*, and back to *"We"* again.

The expressions of our mature and immature work in a very similar way. For as long as we are here, living in duality with other human beings, we are going to need to go into our immature self to keep evolution moving forward. But on a more basic level, to keep conversations and friendships moving forward, the aim of using the polarity framework is not to live in our mature the whole time, but to make our immature healthy. To make our desires and intentions healthy, keeping a clear sense of balance and duality in our life. Our mature evolves from the immature, so the more we know and understand the immature, *and often more importantly, our shadow,* then the more depth there is to our mature.

Example

A woman may grow up to be very accomplished and self-aware, but when she looks to her immature feminine traits, they are simply not very present, neither her healthy or unhealthy ones. The masculine, both mature and immature, might be overdeveloped, compensating for the lack of immature feminine, and this makes it almost impossible for this woman to develop and take her mature feminine traits to the next level.

The immature feminine is likely to be prominent in her life through external sources, as life mirrors to us what we strongly reject and resist through others. So, the more we reject or resist something inside of ourselves, the more we see it outside or in some cases, the more we desire it, in a guilty, and shameful way. Perhaps through her daughter or friends, the immature feminine is creating problems in her life, but she also sees that in the lives of others, the immature feminine brings success, regardless of how she judges their acquired success. By gossiping, being the centre of attention, being dramatic, cathartic, and crying a lot, both the daughter and her friends seem to get what they want. The most helpful thing that this woman can do, is to find ways to welcome in her immature feminine, because without it, her mature feminine will struggle to create depth, have empathy, inspiration, or be creative.

The lack of Femininity means, that through polarity and duality, her masculine also suffers: her mature masculine will not be able to grow beyond a certain point because his growth has to be in relation to the feminine's expressions. For his balance between logical and emotional information to evolve, he needs to experience the deeper levels of feminine creativity and intuition.

This is not the easiest therapy in the world, fears and real risks can come up. For instance this woman might be very adept in using the law of attraction and thus experiences fear of attracting negative drama into her life by desiring it. She is desiring it in order to heal her immature feminine, but she fears attracting accidents, harming those she loves, or even worse, through role-playing her drama in a transformative way, or she might get so lost in her immature feminine that she makes illogical and bad decisions. The immature masculine is likely to rationalize the concept of developing the immature feminine away, because paradoxical answers are hard for him to understand.

The best chance that this woman has of correcting the problems in her life, is exaggerating, and playing with her immature feminine, bringing it out in a conscious way. The healthy and unhealthy, the dark, the light, and the shadow. This will give her a better understanding of herself and others and she will also find it easier to be with her friends and make new ones because she is more accepting of their immature feminine flaws, the ones she was previously rejecting in herself. She will also have developed new depths of compassion and empathy, through this process of embodying the immature feminine.

Each moment that a sense of victimhood arises, instead of immediately following the polarity framework in the conventional way—*being wise and discerning; taking responsibility; holding space and boundaries from her mature masculine*—this woman could first try to play with and embody her emotion of victimhood without actually ever needing to "be" a victim. Her experiences of victimhood need more information and depth in them to evolve into the mature feminine so she needs to give this area of her life more space and energy.

Creativity is built on the transcendence of victimhood. By understanding victimhood and anxiousness in the immature feminine, the mature feminine has access to more empathy, freedom, trust, and creativity. Another way to say this, is that, "we suffer for our passions".

The above statement relates to the woman in our example, as she is informed by, has an experience of, and more understanding for the immature polarity, even though she is no longer focusing on it. However if she's never really focused on it, then spending time in her immature feminine and learning to *"suffer for her passions"* from this place in an unharmful and almost joyful way, would be the wisest thing she could do. Healthier ways to relate to our own experiences of victimhood are covered later, because like it or not, this is simply a part of life and as we develop more understanding around victimhood it becomes easier for us to use and channel our energy into more mature ways of being. The woman in our example could also play with the desire to gossip, something she's always judged as bad, by:

- noticing what energy and outcomes are created by nurturing and acting upon this "negative" desire to gossip;
- and how later, there is a "positive" impact that would otherwise not have been found.

The above two questions are controversial and crucially, thought provoking, but when we need more health and depth in our life, we should look for "negative", immature actions that do no real harm, are not malicious, but still create energy, that we can use to bring about positive change in our life and in the world. Whenever there is a desire to manipulate, seduce, or be cathartic, this woman would benefit from exploring it and working with her mental programming until she desires the power to seduce and the emotional rush of being cathartic.

Learning how to create and increase emotional energy within ourselves is a powerful tool and life skill. Maybe she decides to manipulate, seduce, and flirt with a man or her husband, using his healthy desires to control him so in the end, he gets something that he really wants and needs. Again, this book is not saying that this is good, right, or even okay, but potentially needed and the only way for this woman to feel good, right and okay. For most of us, this is what our subconscious mind is doing all of the time anyway, but generally, through unhealthy means as we are unconscious to the fact that we are doing it.

If this woman loves dogs but knows she does not have time for one due to work and other commitments, she might decide to go home and tell her husband that she wants a puppy. She needs to become completely attached to the emotion and desire of wanting a puppy to start an argument and go into the drama of wanting something and someone else not letting you have it. *Generally, at some point it's good to let people know that you're doing this and why, otherwise you might be gifted with a puppy.*

To role-play with the desire of wanting a puppy to an extreme for several days, would give this woman information about the immature feminine that she lacks and needs. For her to feel a lack of freedom on the emotional level, to feel resistance and restraint gives her the information and energy to direct into something else.

11
A Note on Judgement

Judgements are not bad but immature, *and being immature is essential for our evolution.* To notice when we are acting from our immature could be seen as a judgement, but there is a difference between seeing something for what it is and judging it.

Knowing is a higher vibration of discernment and discernment *(earned truth),* is a higher vibration of judgement. Judgement, discernment, and knowing are all actually one and the same; it is the vibration that is different. When we use discernment, we are choosing from what is known to us. This means that we have already learned lessons about judgement and other immature traits. Or we are tapping into the wisdom of previous generations: friends, teachers, and people we trusted to influence our lives.

When our actions and choices feel as if they come from a higher perspective, with no effort or thought on our part, it is because we have learned our immature lessons. We have integrated our immature. We have created enough *alignment* within our physical, mental, and emotional bodies that we just "know" what is true for us at any specific time. This is why it's so important to know that truth can change, that what is right and true in one moment, might not be so in another. The immature mind and the unhealthy ego can find knowing a truth that can change at any moment, hard to accept. But with practice, we can prove to ourselves that this is . . . *true.* Inner knowing comes from the other 90% of our being, that is not our conscious, logical mind, and often not our subconscious mind either.

The more self-trust we develop, the more access we have to the unconscious: *what we don't already know.* We evolve when we make the unconscious and subconscious, conscious. *It's helpful to remember that the more conscious we become, the more our own unconscious behaviours hurt us.* As we become more aware and sensitive it's important to have good grounding and strong foundations that allow us to experience sensitivity without excess suffering.

There is always a danger of arrogance and fake spiritual maturity when we apply "discernment" or "knowing" to a situation, but the more authentic we are with ourselves, and the more accepting of our flaws, the less the danger. We must trust that we know the difference between lying to ourselves or thinking that we know, and knowing.

12

The Good, the Bad, the Healthy, and the Unhealthy

It's almost impossible to explore the paradox of duality and polarity without creating contradictions. As discussed, good and bad are not really truths but judgements, and shifting our mind away from the judgements of good and bad is one of the most powerful shifts the human mind can take. But we still need to use some form of language to help us navigate duality, so we use healthy and unhealthy. Healthy is not good and it's not bad. Too much coffee is unhealthy for the gut, but sometimes it's exactly what we need to succeed at an important task or to not fall asleep while driving a car. The scientifically healthy option from a reductionist point of view can often have the worst consequences: everything is relative to our circumstance and what we desire.

Polarity and duality work best when they are interchangeable and flexible. We could say that the mature and immature are polarity and that masculine and feminine are duality, but sometimes it is helpful for our mind to grasp a concept by saying it the other way round, especially when we include the healthy, unhealthy, and shadow dynamics. We can easily constrict and limit ourselves with language and this is not always helpful. In relation to the framework, it's more helpful to allow everything to change and alternate around the four quadrants, not fully labelling anything as something.

Even expressing polarities and dualities as *concepts*, and the masculine, feminine, mature, immature, healthy and unhealthy as *traits* is restrictive, they are the fundamental building blocks of our emotional reality and they have to be flexible and interchangeable for reality to work, so even restricting them under the labels of *"concepts and traits"*, is not helpful, just like it's not helpful to label or restrict a human being with definitive terms such as, *"you are . . ."*, it is normally always better to communicate with a person by saying, *"you're being . . ."*

It can sometimes be helpful to visualize the framework as a spiral and each time we circle through the framework, we create more or less depth. The framework itself is purposely expressed as a two-dimensional square with four quadrants, because it is expressing the paradox of reality which moves through time in a more circular and spiralling fashion, with a fractal nature. The polarity framework simplifies reality to a basic pattern of polarity and duality that needs to keep constantly changing places with itself for life to happen.

Mindfulness and removing strict language constraints, support us to recognize unconscious reactive behaviour, pre-programmed judgements, past conditioning, and helps us apply our free will. It is not simply a practice of changing words around in our head, because then we will continue to judge; we are changing the meaning of *bad,* so that bad becomes a tool for us to work with polarity and we are changing our subconscious response to language, to help us realize that sometimes bad is good, that the wrong thing can change and turn into the right thing an hour later. Most of us know this to be true, but it is not at the forefront of our mind, so we do not use this knowledge, especially in times of fear and stress, when this knowledge is needed the most.

Instead, many of us use our pre-programmed judgements and reactive behaviour, making ourselves unable to change the fractal patterns of our life.

13
Catch-22: No Model for the Mature

~

The phrase Catch-22 is used when the attempt to escape makes escape impossible.

"I need my mature feminine to evolve my masculine, but I don't feel I have it. And I need my mature masculine to evolve my feminine, but I don't feel that I have that either."

We all have both the mature and immature, as well as access to our higher self: our uniqueness comes from how we develop them. If we have one, then we must have the other, as this is the law of polarity; it may feel dormant, but our mature side must be there. What can be hard is getting out of our own *reactive behaviour* enough to embody it, but the more we do so, the more our mature develops.

Note: Not all of the options below use the standard approach of using the polarity framework, which is:

Embodying: the opposing mature.
Evolving: into the mature of that same polarity.
Avoiding: the opposing immature.

When in a catch 22 situation, we need to find our own best way of working with the framework. It's good to read through all of these options with the mirror map to gain a deeper understanding of how to work when feeling stuck.

Example: If we *identify with anxious behaviour in the immature feminine,* but responsibility, holding space, and boundaries from our mature masculine feels alien to us, then moving into our feminine, trusting nature, can be difficult.

Option 1

The opposing immature: *avoidance* opposes *anxiousness*. If being *avoidant* is not a problem for us, we can simply focus on being even less *avoidant*. By default, this will move us from our immature masculine *(avoidance),* into our mature masculine of *responsibility, holding space, and boundaries.* We will simply start to demonstrate the mature traits that we did not feel we had.

From here, it becomes much easier to work on our original issue of *anxiety.*

To summarize: if the opposing immature trait is not an issue for us, instead of avoiding it as normal, we can make our main focus to be *less* of this trait, *without being anything else.* So, if my issue is in the immature feminine, I can actively focus on making my immature masculine less *without* simultaneously making anything else more, and this will support my evolution to the mature and overall health on the framework *(this slightly contradicts previous advice on how to use the polarity framework but the framework is paradoxical in nature, as is life, so instead of arguing about the contradictions of life, it's much more enlightening to understand why they are there).*

Option 2

If *anxiousness* is the main problem, but being *avoidant* is also a problem, we can solve it by emphasizing our *avoidance.*

If we start to purposefully act in the other immature, the one we have "less" of a problem with, in this case our immature masculine, then we need the mature feminine *(instead of the mature masculine which we did not feel was attainable),* to solve our problem.

(Take a breath, otherwise this gets complicated.)

Focusing on the *Freedom and Trust* that we already have to some degree (the polarity of *anxiousness*), will support our immature masculine to become mature, to become *responsible.* Now it is so much easier to deal with our original problem of *anxiousness,* because we are strengthening our memories of being *responsible.*

If you're also struggling to identify with *Freedom and Trust* (the polarity of the immature trait you're working on), write a list of your freedoms, *"I'm free to walk in the park, speak my mind, file a petition to Government . . .",* or whatever collective freedoms you have in your country and then write a list of what you trust, *"I trust that my dog loves me, I trust myself to drive a car, to cook amazing pasta . . ."* Just start small and work your way up, developing the opposing mature trait to the one that solves your current issue.

To summarize: when *anxiousness* is our focus, *Freedom and Trust* are simply less attainable. So, when the immature feminine is our focus, the mature feminine is less attainable. By changing our focus to a different problem, by default we can create the solution to our original problem, and to do this we create more of a problem than we really have in the opposing immature, which helps develop the mature of the same polarity related to our problem, which in turn develops the opposing mature, which has the traits we need to solve our original unhealthy immature issue.

This might sound complicated but it's not; once we focus on something, we start to have it, mature or immature. One expression of the mature will always lead to an opposing expression of the other mature for as long as we seek balance and integration within our lives.

Exercise

Run options 1 and 2 above through the maps using different scenarios of your choosing, in the same way as we did for the example, *identifying with anxious behaviour in the immature feminine.* This exercise really does help in learning to use the framework, making it subconscious, and deepening our understanding.

If you feel that you don't have access to enough of your mature traits to work with your issue on the polarity framework, the next seven options can help. If you find reading specific advice too preachy and controlling and prefer to find your own way, feel free to skip ahead to the next chapter.

Option 3

Take smaller steps. If we don't already have a model or any way of drawing from and developing responsibility and holding clear boundaries, we can make it a goal and aim for it. Starting with our original example, *Lack of mature masculine—lack of responsibility, holding space and boundaries:*

- write down what you already encompass, what people can rely on you for, the traits that you already have and what you appreciate about yourself in relation to all of the mature masculine traits;
- or write down the boundaries that you hold well;
- remember times that you said yes, but meant no, and look to changing this behaviour. Honouring our yes, and honouring our no is crucial—these words are very important.

It's basically a case of knowing it is possible, creating an intention and commitment and then going for it, with as much creativity as possible.

Another example is, if we often feel like a victim and have issues expressing wisdom and discernment, we can look at ways to develop our wisdom. Books and role models will teach us so much, but it's in applying these lessons in different situations that wisdom is attained. Just deeply understanding the concept of discernment and how it differs from judgement, gets our mind ready to use discernment and to be discerning more often, thus we will automatically *judge less.*

Or, if it's being passive-aggressive and not knowing what selflessness looks like, we might try taking up meditation or finding one of the many Eastern practices that supports realizing selflessness, such as yoga or applied correctly, martial arts.

Option 4

Develop the mature traits that we already have, as they all support each other. If demonstrating masculine responsibility is hard, we can work on other masculine traits, such as mindfulness, discernment, emotional and mental balance, and interdependence. Eventually, this will increase our ability to act from the mature masculine traits that we feel we are lacking in, which in this case is responsibility.

Option 5

Find a good bodywork practitioner, someone who can help work with traumas and cellular vibrations on the physical, emotional and mental levels. There are so many different therapies and therapists out there, it is important to find someone who works for you. It's often the individual person's sense of self, their life experiences and ego that serves us more than what they actually trained in or have qualifications for. Of course, good and proper training is important too, but many trainings miss the important points and over-teach on others to ensure an income, rarely failing students. Thus, when working emotionally and with the body in a non-intrusive way, it's normally better to opt for someone we feel good with, opposed to a person with many qualifications.

The best way to *"learn"* something is often to *"learn to teach"* something. So, doing a therapy-related training with no interest in actually qualifying or practising as a therapist is often one of the best ways to heal ourselves. Fortunately, there are many courses and workshops now that consider this and offer the middle ground. *Kundalini Bodywork utilizes the integrative therapy practices of de-armouring, breathwork, and energetic bodywork, with the polarity framework in a way that is inclusive of our sexuality* but it's important to find a modality and training format that works for you.

I personally find combining Western psychology with Eastern, mainly Taoist and Tantric practices, that include sexuality, is the best way to change the vibration of the body and to heal holistically. This is the path that I follow through Kundalini Bodywork with a focus on shadow and energetic bodywork practices.

Option 6

Adopting a role model is not my preferred way of working but it helps some people. Write down all of the traits that you admire in such a person that will help you overcome the issues you're currently working on. And then embody these traits and make them your own. *Do not embody the other person's ego;* don't try to be someone else. Being yourself and loving yourself for who you are is important. Striving towards a better version of yourself is always the best choice.

Option 7

Developing our will power, psychic, and extra-sensory perceptions, gives greater access to the knowledge within. Practitioners in methodologies such as hypnosis, working with Akashic records, lucid dreaming, and other reputable, alternative/holistic approaches to develop extra-sensory perception can all help. It's best to go with the method that attracts you the most.

Option 8

Sometimes it's good to talk with a more mainstream therapist or counsellor so when we need help we should ask for it. It's also important to understand that any form of help that does not lead to us finding our own answers, our own cures, and healing our self is normally on one level incomplete, but in the mid-term may be the best solution for us. A good counsellor would and should always lead us to finding our own answers, or at the very least embodying and owning the answers that we agree to as our own.

Option 9

Some people like to take the, "fake it until you make it", approach. This can work, but we need to be careful when doing so, as too many positive affirmations with inauthenticity can hurt us and create a larger shadow. We need balanced growth so I would generally steer clear of this option when possible or apply it with moderation.

This list is by no means exhaustive so please feel free to add to it and reach out to other professionals and other sources when you need to develop more healthy and mature traits within yourself, and help evolve the immature traits that you feel stuck in.

14

The Mature and Immature Archetypes of Parenthood

It's important to reiterate here that masculine and feminine are not bound by gender and as we explore the archetypes of the:

- immature mother
- immature father
- mature mother
- mature father

to remember that these archetypes are in both men and women as well as children. It's simpler for us to explore them with men in the fathering role and women in the mothering role, but many people will recognize their own mother, even if very feminine, as often being in her masculine energy. When reflecting on your life in relation to these archetypes, try not to restrict yourself too much with gender or biology, but pay more attention to who and what influenced you.

Demonstrating the mature masculine in an immature society is difficult. Currently most, if not all of society, fundamentally goes against what the mature masculine is here to teach. The influence of the immature masculine is everywhere: school, TV, media, music, advertising, time management, and the financial system. The immature masculine is the fabric of our cultures and societies.

Children need to develop their immature selves as they create their sense of separate self and we all need models for the healthy immature, no matter our age. It's hard for all aspects of our immature to be expressed as healthy, but as we've discussed, we need to avoid judgements of good, bad, right, wrong, and evil. Even our unhealthy immature has moments in life where it serves the best, but as we choose to consciously evolve, these moments become less.

Fortunately, when the mature masculine father is fully present, no matter to whom he is talking and listening to, he is hard to ignore. Teenage sons for example, can be a challenge, feelings of unworthiness might come up for the father, and competition between father and son can arise. A man acting from his immature masculine may try to stop his son's growth if he is feeling a lack of power. This dynamic might show as the Father trying to rescue his son, when his son does not need rescuing, putting him down verbally or finishing his sentences in an attempt to feel some kind of fake power in that he has things under control. Clearly, this energy is not limited to fatherhood, or men, and if we find ourselves or others doing this, we need to not judge too harshly, as the judgements create more immature expressions within us and within the people around us.

The mature masculine father takes responsibility for everything in his environment. Acting from the perspective that life is a mirror, if his children are angry, he might take action in the moment, but afterwards he will look within. He will ask what is going on in his internal world that has created anger in their internal or external world. This might sound like an extreme approach, but the mature masculine father will always take responsibility for the world around him, from the perspective that life is a mirror. He will still hold others accountable for their actions, but from the meta perspective, he knows their actions are his lessons and are created by his thoughts, feelings, conscious, and subconscious intentions.

As his children grow up and learn to use their inner power, he does not suddenly feel inadequate, the mature father is integrated and his inner feminine is self-assured. He does not need validation, he knows who he is, and he understands life, he understands that by taking responsibility for everything, even things which seem out of his control, such as politics and war, he is accepting his interconnectedness to life, to everything that is. It's in this interconnectedness that he has the power to change the world for the better as he sees fit and with his free will.

In the masculine, one of the most important lessons that both the mature and immature father teaches us, is how to fight. The immature father wants to keep us down and thus gives us something to fight against, while the mature father brings us up knowing what is right and just, thus giving us something to fight for. As we become more mature and develop higher perspectives, we can see beyond unhealthy competitiveness and fighting. But for most people, fighting is about creating identity and a sense of self, our ego: whether it ends up healthy or unhealthy. We see this in small children and toddlers as they start to realize a sense of separate self, fondly calling it the "terrible twos".

From the feminine's perspective, we can be so emphatic and welcoming that we lose ourselves in the energy of others, temporarily cutting ourselves off from our own uniqueness and inner truth. This is why it's important to know who we are through the eyes of the masculine. Knowing and owning our masculine traits and our individual expression, while simultaneously being in our feminine energy, means we can act in alignment with our higher self.

The mature feminine as the archetype of motherhood is completely loving, caring, and accepting. In sickness and harder times, she can love even more intensely and requires very little in return. The immature mother is often acting from lack and a fear-based consciousness; it could be fear that she is not good enough or fear that she will be left alone, and this can make the immature mother manipulative. Both consciously and unconsciously creating mini traumas in her children and the people around her. These mini traumas create negative thoughts and behavioural patterns which, if we don't learn from them, will keep us locked in our unhealthy ego, reacting from fear and moving us further into unconscious separation. But if we do learn from them, understanding the polarity and duality of the situation, we develop and can create new, mature behavioural thoughts and patterns.

Sometimes it is the worst things that the feminine does to us that hold the greatest gifts. This can be an actual mother, a wife, a friend, or even a man, acting from his feminine. People who choose to heal and work on themselves, can end up having some of the most interesting, loving, and diverse personalities, regardless of their childhoods. Both the mature and immature mother want to make sure that we grow into diverse individuals, full of life experience. The immature does this from a place of fear, possibly manipulating, creating trauma and pain, while the mature does it from a place of love, working in co-creation with us, listening to our desires and creating all the rich and fruitful experiences for us that she can from her own life experiences and understandings. *For the feminine, it's a process of transmutation, as she creates her children's future from her past.*

The important thing to remember when using Masculine and Feminine Polarity Work, is not to get attached to the words themselves. Words are fluid and language is an expression of the feminine, they can speak great truth but they can also be manipulative. Everything is a partial truth and most truths have another truth directly contradicting them, this concept must be grasped and embodied by our immature masculine in order for evolution to occur.

Healing Our Mother and Father Issues through Their Archetypes

As we try to heal our mother and father issues, it can be easy to get lost in our personal history and the story of our life, what our parents and guardians did or did not do. We may have inherited negative beliefs or personality conditionings that are not true for us, such as:

- "Everyone abandons me."
- "I'm not lovable."
- "The world is cruel."
- "To be loved I need to be successful, follow rules, be pretty, be quiet, beat other children at sports" or whatever narrative we adopted in our childhood.

If we get too wrapped up in our story and blame others for our life, we miss the bigger picture and we don't get to learn and grow from our pain. We need to see the story as a means to experience more of life, instead of being our life.

Both the immature masculine and feminine and the immature mother and father will continue to propagate a culture of blaming and shaming and a society based on power-over thinking opposed to power-with, until we as a collective move into more mature ways of being, governing, and parenting ourselves from this place. Immature traits are currently embedded in our values and culture in the same way that our mother and father are embedded into us, giving us our imprint of masculinity and femininity. When the immature collectively dominates in this way, we create a society where the gap between the haves and have nots, the rich and the poor, can only get bigger. For our immature traits to be healthy they need to be balanced and integrated with our mature, then our immature traits become very positive.

Before we can heal these cultural traits, we need to heal the immature within ourselves using polarity and duality. And to do this, we need to look at the archetypal roles of mother and father, in both the mature and immature. It is from these that we inherit our imprint for the masculine and feminine and our initial concept of what it means to be mature.

By developing our inner mother and father at a higher vibrational level, with more depth and understanding, we pass on an evolved imprint to the next generation. The more we understand how polarity and duality work, the more discernment we develop, choosing how we experience life, moment to moment. By de-personalizing our own mother and father from the archetypal roles of the mature and immature mother and father, we have a much greater chance of healing ourselves and society. As well as de-personalizing from our story and trauma, the story and trauma of our parents and that of our culture, we also need to accept that seemingly *"bad"* things happen and learn to judge these seemingly *good* and *bad* things less.

Our unhealthy ego's primary purpose is to keep us in separation, to stop us from realizing our complete interconnectedness to all life and the power that comes with this. It achieves this by judging things as good and bad from a limited perspective and uses these judgements to perpetuate the story of our life, our suffering, and what we need to be afraid of.

The unhealthy ego will continue to succeed, generation after generation, for as long as we reject what we judge as bad and see it as out there and in other people instead of within us. We need to have both an intellectual understanding and emotional acceptance of our inner processes and our inner immaturity before we can begin to transform ourselves.

It's important to remember that sometimes things go wrong in life and unfortunate, and tragic things happen. Wars still happen, slavery is still real, people get sick, and babies still die. But for the majority of us, over our entire lifetime, unfortunate and tragic events that are not in alignment with our personal vibration are rare. Most problems and painful experiences are a mix of the collective consciousness expressing what is, and our personal vibrational frequency being reflected back to us by the law of attraction.

For people who have been treated very badly to say, "that they attracted it", can sound unacceptable, but when we are a baby, we are vulnerable, helpless, and we have no choice but to accept the vibrations of the people around us. We cannot fully exercise our free will because we cannot say "no", or walk away. Unconsciously, we pick up vibrations such as abuse and neglect from people around us, that lead us later in life to attracting abuse, neglect, and feelings of unlovability, or whatever it is that we feel we have, but never chose or said yes to.

Being bullied; being victimized; losing at sports; losing friends; losing at school, and losing in life; living in the shadow of our mother; or supporting the narcissist ego of our father. In each case on the subconscious level, we are asking them to be this for us and on an even deeper level, it is actually a part of our inner masculine or feminine that is doing it to us. We are all doing it *all* to ourselves, and we will continue to do so for as long as it feels familiar and is a vibrational match for how we consciously and subconsciously feel.

If vibrations were forced on to us when we were very small, before we could demonstrate free will and before we could speak, then later in life all we can do is attract and recreate similar patterns, until we come to a place where our free will is strong enough and our life conditions supportive enough that we can change and break our past conditioning.

Taking responsibility for the painful experiences of our life, does not mean that we are guilty and our abusers innocent. It means, on the deepest level, that once we exercise free will and heal our traumas: physically, emotionally and mentally, we are able to take our power back, controlling our life with the vibrations we choose. We can only fully take back our power when we forgive both them and ourselves for creating the situation. We move from victimhood *(immature feminine),* into creative power *(mature feminine)* when we release our judgements *(immature masculine)* and take full responsibility for our life *(mature masculine).* When seemingly bad things happen regardless of our vibration, we need to remember that a higher vibration equals less of these seemingly bad things.

By not judging our situation and experiences as good or bad, but by authentically feeling the emotions that they create, our pain can become pleasurable, a long cry can feel really good. When we judge less without attachment, our vibration is higher and things don't hurt so much. The most painful thing about pain, is the rejection of it; rejected and suppressed pain will eventually turn into numbness, a physical and emotional numbness that leaves us dead inside. Realizing that how our parents treated us was a reflection of how we felt inside at the time and each time they acted in this way our "negative" feelings were reinforced so we attracted more of the same, is actually one of the most empowering realizations that we can have: *It is saying that I am the master of my reality.*

This realization comes from the mature masculine taking responsibility and encompassing as much of reality as he can. The law of attraction is working on a subconscious level and in total relationship with our environment. It's not about beating ourselves up, blaming, and shaming ourselves or others for the reality we are co-creating. There just comes a moment when we need to break the cycle and to start working for change in the collective consciousness.

For areas in the world where war or slavery is sadly still a regular occurrence, then to change this pattern we need to work on the global governance issues that support it, *allowing the mature masculine to lead more than he currently is,* helping people on an individual level, to judge less and raise their vibration so they no longer attract it.

Working on the individual level for ourselves and with others is not always easy and takes more than just understanding the concepts on a mental level. We need to go through the process and feel our feelings, we need to release and forgive the old patterning on the physical, mental, and emotional levels and then we need to integrate the new vibrations into these three levels of our being. When we do this, we release the emotional and physical triggers that bring up our feelings of abandonment, lack of love, needing to please, fight, compete, or whatever else relates to our childhood.

We may never be fully healed and *some would say that continually healing and learning from pain is an essential part of life, but whatever we believe, we certainly need to go through this cycle several times before professionally helping others with their parental issues in this way.*

Becoming Our Own Parents

As we self-realize, we see that all of the masculine and feminine archetypes and roles are within us. In some moments, we are the mother, in others the father, later the child, the sister, and the brother. Whether it's a small boy mothering others or a female friend acting from the father, we are all constantly playing these roles for each other. As we do this, we might be unconsciously following a healthy or an unhealthy behavioural pattern, but the more conscious we are of these major archetypes, the more mature and healthy our behaviours become.

If we felt unloved by our mother, then we might act "needy" in our relationships, with our inner feminine acting from her immature and seeking attention or perhaps we treat others coldly when they need mothering or maybe we smother them with love as an expression of our own neediness. The results from any childhood are layers and layers of polarity and duality, weaving through our emotional, mental and physical bodies, making up the unique and intricate personalities of each of us, however we turn out.

In regard to parenthood, maybe we become the opposite of who we judged our parents to be, or maybe we find ourselves copying our parents' reactive, trauma-fuelled behaviour. Often it will be a mixture, meaning that in part, we will become the thing that we despise and we will continue to be so until we accept it as part of ourselves and forgive ourselves for creating it.

We created it via the law of attraction or the law of resistance, *which is basically the same thing,* because whether we are actively resisting or attracting something, we are focusing on it, be it consciously or subconsciously.

When we learn to embody the archetypes of the mature mother and mature father within ourselves, we will recognize that in its greatest sense, *the laws of attraction and polarity have always been and will always be parenting us, thus we parent ourselves through diverse spectrums of emotional vibrations.* This can sound sad and lonely, but ultimately it is liberating, and frees us for a greater understanding of life. When we can accept that we are all the roles and we play all of the roles, we are much closer to liberation.

Ultimately, there is only one masculine and one feminine, and they are both inside of us. Every relationship and interaction we have is a relationship and interaction with ourselves. *If we need to forgive our parents, we also need to forgive ourselves.* When we take responsibility for the whole, we see beyond our sense of separate self and we see that we are limitless and we are timeless. In this sense, we can see that age does not matter, we will always have the mother, the father, the child, the sister and the brother, within us.

When we can embody what we feel another did to us as if we did it to ourselves, *taking on their role as the perpetrator when we were the victim* and then forgiving ourselves for whatever it was that we did to ourselves *(they did to us),* then we have recognized our potential to hurt others and to do harm and we have learned from it, from both sides.

Using Masculine and Feminine Polarity Work to this extent, on such a *non-dualist level,* is quite advanced and can be hard. It's good to have the help of professionals and trusted friends when dealing with our issues.

If forgiveness on this level feels impossible, just forgive as much as is authentic. Lying to ourselves or denying our feelings because we understand the intellect of something, but lack the emotional intelligence to integrate our feelings, is very damaging and unhealthy behaviour.

The only way to get to a place of having enough emotional intelligence in order to accept how we feel, is to be authentic about how we feel.

Parenting with Masculine and Feminine Polarity Work

When applying Masculine and Feminine Polarity Work to parenting, it's important to remember that children need all of our sides. They need the mature masculine and feminine and the immature masculine and feminine.

And they need these expressions to be shown from all the major influences in their lives. A completely masculine father and feminine mother is just not sustainable, feasible, or healthy. Ideally, children need to see healthy demonstrations of the aligned and integrated self, showing up in their daily life. They need to learn and grow by experiencing adults and other children in an authentic way. Children learn and develop their egos largely through their own and our mistakes. We could be the most loving and providing parent in the world, but unwillingly and unconsciously, most if not all parents, will at some point traumatize their children and we have to find a way to be okay with this and forgive ourselves for their benefit as well as our own.

Ours and our children's pain and trauma have the potential to turn into some of our and their greatest gifts and teachers in later life. For many, it's what shapes our personality because our mind is trained to remember the *"bad"* more than *"good"*, so we do not get hurt again. By learning to use polarity and duality in our own self-development, we give our children the best chance of using it in theirs, turning their trauma and negative life experiences into gifts, instead of self-destructive patterns.

Once our mind has moved beyond the judgements of good and bad, and can still be authentic to our own truth and our own growth within the constraints of our personality and ego, then we have already come a long way in understanding and mastering duality. To think that we know it all or understand something fully *(understand it from every dimension of space and time, and time and space)* would be arrogant. From our conscious mind's perspective, we can never know it all, but the more humble and grateful that we can be *(mature masculine)*, the more we will know, and also the more we can understand and communicate with both our subconscious mind and our higher selves *(which our mature masculine and feminine gives us access to)*, the more we will know.

Our inner mother and her expressions of mature and immature traits, will normally be a mix of our genetic mother and the female person that we felt the most cared for by in our younger life, if this is different. Although not a rule, but just like our physicality, many of our personality traits and unconscious behaviours are inherited through our DNA. If the mother, the woman, is very masculine, then often the child is likely to grow up to be a masculine kind of mother despite how they are in the rest of their lives. But as this book explains, set rules don't work well on a dualistic level because life is a paradox and we all have free will, so we may choose something else, choose to be different, to rebel and resist when the norm is to conform, to follow and attract in life the same things that our parents did.

Polarity, duality and the law of attraction, are always working with our free will and intention: understanding how these basic building blocks of life shape us and our children, gives us a far better chance of creating a future that they love. Maybe our children match our behaviours and values or maybe they do the opposite, rejecting them, rejecting us and what we want for them. Or maybe they manage to heal and integrate the polarities that they inherited from us, creating a healthy and balanced personality that expresses their authentic aligned self (which is the best that we can all hope for).

Some common themes and outcomes that we may recognize within ourselves are:

- Our mother had a very healthy, mature feminine, creative personality, so we developed one too.
- Our mother had a very healthy, mature feminine, creative personality, so we developed more of the opposing masculine and became wise and discerning, much more likely if there is no father figure present, so the child plays the polarity to balance her energy.
- Our mother had an unhealthy, mature feminine, creative personality, so we became the polarity of this, moving into victimhood or one of the other immature feminine traits. Alternatively, maybe we moved into our immature masculine to cope with her unhealthy false self-image and became very critical and judgemental of her, a valid and needed defence to an unhealthy mature feminine.
- Or maybe we are a rarity in this world, so self-assured within our own being and with such strong will and purpose, that we only ever follow our own soul's and higher self's advice. We are less likely to be consumed by the negative and lower vibrations of others, because we find natural alignment easily, so can easily listen to our higher self.

We are all multi-faceted with preferred unconscious and conscious patterns and ways of beings, it is likely that all of the above listed things are true for us to some degree. We should always know that our higher self, our soul, the small voice within or however we choose to call it, is there and the more alignment we have between our three main bodies, the more we can listen, leaving behind the unconscious conditioning of our parents and thus, passing less unconscious conditioning onto our children.

15
Working with Our Inner Critic

Expressions of our inner critic can be quite personal and our relationship with it may need to change over time. Created from our personal psychology, fundamentally it is an expression of polarity, but often it is polarity experienced in an unhealthy way.

For most of us it is active:

- when we are unhappy;
- and when we do not feel enough balance or safety in our life: this can also relate to feeling "too" happy, so a lack of balance or unfamiliarity, thus a lack of safety. Remember, that we are all unique, so if the statement about being "too happy" seems un-comprehensible to you this is okay.

Our inner critic serves two main functions, depending on how we look at it, if we are vibrating more from love or fear, more from our mature or immature.

It might:

- perpetuate our suffering, keeping conscious awareness locked in the mind with familiar patterns of negativity that eventually reduce our use of free will, leaving us repeatedly choosing negative options through familiarity and repetition;
- or encourage us to destroy old energy by criticizing the old way of being, thus giving us new energy to create new life with.

In the second instance, our inner critic or self-saboteur, is here to destroy something: to create enough chaos in our life so that we have enough energy to create what we want. Or enough negative, lower vibrational energy to put us back into a state of balance. It is often viewed as a form of self-destructive behaviour, but when we understand our inner critic and our relationship with it, we can begin to change our experience of it and stop judging our inner critic as *"bad"* all of the time, accepting it is how it is right now.

When we notice the voice of our inner critic instead of *"only ever"* or *"just"* overriding it with self-discipline, we would be wise to ask questions like:

- what am I afraid of?
- where is my life out of balance?

If self-destructive behaviours emerge, we should look where our life is currently not going in a direction that we want. Not necessarily in an unhealthy direction, just not our highest and our best. But if our inner critic is attacking the highest and best in our life, then we should look to see where we are out of balance and where we are underdeveloped in other areas of our life. When we have balance in our life and are working with our masculine and feminine in a healthy way, our inner critic will not be present.

Polarity, tension and conflict are essential for the dualistic reality that we live in. We need tension in our lives to create new experiences and we need the polarity of masculine and feminine within ourselves to create life outside of ourselves. Where our inner critic is concerned, we need to know if we are simply not applying enough discipline to reach our goals and need to work more with a fighting kind of energy, being in creative conflict with more tension, while being grateful that our inner critic is there giving us someone or something to push against and drive us forward.

As we remove the need to judge and are able to act from discernment and knowingness, then our inner critic starts to transform and for each person this can be different. Instead of feeling bad about our inner critic or trying to change it with our mind, we can see it for what it really is and what it has the potential to be. *Our inner critic is the part of us that looks to make energy from destruction in order to create something new.* The desire to destroy life is the lower vibration of the desire to create life, *ultimately* it is the same desire.

When we fully understand ourselves, we realize that the desires to create and destroy are simply both a desire for life.

It's only in our unhealthy immature states that our inner critic is damaging to us. So, when this happens, we need to see it as a reminder to look at what is unhealthy in our life. When we can see and know this, we can find ways to channel our inner critic: the destroyer in us, to work with the creator in us, allowing us to find the mature masculine's win-win scenario in almost every situation, even the ones we consciously choose to destroy.

Being heavily critical of others or having an inner critic who is too negative and out of control will not serve us, so we need to evolve our immature. If our inner critic or outer critic is extreme, then these next two techniques can be helpful: neither is the right way, different ways simply serve us better at different times.

Gratitude

Look at what we are critical of within ourselves and see where we can find gratitude for it, no matter how silly or small:

- I'm grateful that I failed at my diet today because it shows me how severely my body reacts to sugar, tomorrow I will do better, but I love and accept myself completely anyway.
- I'm grateful that my car broke down, because it meant that it had a needed oil change and I got the exercise that I needed. It's taught me to be more responsible and I love and accept myself completely.
- Even though I don't have enough money to buy my children all the things that they want right now, I'm grateful that we have lots of time to spend together and can learn the importance of family. I'm grateful for the money we do have and I love and accept myself completely.

When being grateful for things that we don't want, it's very important to tell ourselves or write down what we do want, followed by, "I love and accept myself completely." Otherwise, we send mixed messages to our subconscious mind and to the universe attracting more of what we do not want.

A very useful skill to learn and develop, is being able to offer constructive criticism to others in a way that they feel gratitude for our input:

- "Hey, I notice that you're working really hard but not getting the results that you want, I want you to be happy, so have you considered . . ." and then finish the sentence as appropriate.
- Or even better, talk with a person so that they find their own answers and feel more empowered, very often people just need to be listened to and encouraged more than given advice.

Impermanence

Impermanence is both the blessing and the curse of the Buddha's, because it means "*everything* changes", good things and bad. But ultimately, self-realization through meditating on impermanence, the impermanence of life, should allow us to transcend suffering, seeing our blessings and our curses as one.

This meditation practice gives many people comfort while still living in duality and enjoying their life. If you really struggle with negative and critical thinking, then notice each time it happens severely enough to create an emotional reaction in you and then sit in meditation for five minutes, breathing deeply into the belly and working with the mantra or repeating in your mind, the phrase:

"Life is impermanent, everything changes, life is impermanent, everything changes . . ."

16
Ending Relationships

When a relationship ends, we are likely to either:

- go through a range of responses in our mature;
- but more often, our immature.

In the immature feminine, we can feel like a victim, like they abused us, we trusted them and then we became hurt. Maybe we feel malicious or maybe our self-destructive nature is triggered because we feel out of balance, illogically craving more abuse due to the law of attraction and because of our feelings of love and gratitude for the person who left us. So, we either abuse ourselves or we attract a similar kind of relationship, in order to relive our story of being a victim.

In the immature masculine, we might want to protect our feminine, so we enter a power struggle, arguing over who left whom, creating stories in our mind of why the other is no good, we build judgement upon judgement trying to justify ourselves. When we enter a new relationship, the immature masculine, is likely to be looking at the balance of power from the start, at how he can suppress their feminine, so his feminine will not feel hurt again.

As we have learnt, we are all integrated mixtures of both the masculine and feminine, but as soon as we can consciously create or recognize this split within ourselves, we can start to observe our behaviours and our actions. Every person, situation, and break up is unique. What will remain the same, is that to move out of our unhealthy immature behaviour, it is always helpful to find the opposing mature behaviour, either within ourselves or elsewhere. Getting our emotions out of the body is very important too, it prevents the experiences and negative vibrations becoming trapped in our body, thus attracting more of the same, painful emotions and experiences. A healthy expression of the immature feminine, through cathartic and overly emotional behaviour, can be a really good thing. It means emotional and mental balance in the mature masculine can follow, because we are not suppressing or rejecting our immature feminine, but allowing her to become healthy.

17
Double Masculine, Double Feminine

You might have noticed that when you and a partner both end up in your masculine, you may both try to lead at the same time, both trying to take care of and control the situation in a domineering way and from the immature: this is where arguments often happen. Very rarely do arguments happen between two people who are in their healthy mature. In the immature, the masculine is normally arguing and the feminine manipulating or playing the victim.

As you evolve as a couple, if you are in a traditional relationship with stereotypical gender roles, you might find when a predominately masculine man, who is feeling very safe starts to open up, he acts more from his feminine, talking in a much more creative and open way where the point is less defined but his creativity and inspiration is exciting. When this happens for periods of several minutes or more, the woman will generally move into her masculine to balance the energy. If for any reason this makes the man uncomfortable, then he is likely to move either into his immature masculine immediately, or first into his immature feminine.

In the second instance, with the man being in his immature feminine, the woman is likely to subconsciously react, polarizing his behaviour by moving into her immature masculine. He is feeling needy, anxious, and seeking attention, while she is feeling avoidant and starts to detach. He may feel uncomfortable with her taking the masculine role, allowing her energy to change him, because:

- She has a lot of unhealthy masculine shadow.
- He is full of fear and too arrogant to let go.
- Or, his higher self simply says no.

In all three of these scenarios, he moves back into his masculine. This can happen quite abruptly and if the woman also stays in her masculine, we have the meeting of two heads, often in the double immature masculine, and arguments are likely to happen. When we understand this dynamic well enough, we are able to see it happening or even better, stop it before it happens. The woman in the example above has multiple choices, two options are:

- be very passive, move into her mature feminine and try to express the lesson that she feels he needs to learn (hoping that he will then move into his mature masculine);
- move into her mature masculine and meet him like a brother, sharing her experience from a place of wisdom to help him see the dynamic that is playing out (hoping that he will then move into his mature masculine so she can move into her feminine, or for him to at least move into his mature feminine, so that they can find a more integrated and non-polarized way of relating).

The different dynamics that can take place between two people are numerous and individual with each party being able to express healthy and unhealthy expressions of the mature and immature in both the masculine and the feminine. Looking at each possible scenario is not so helpful, but understanding how *double masculine and feminine dynamics* work, and show up, is key to a happy life. There is no set way to judge or respond to each dynamic, but having *greater awareness* to how polarities play out and more *self-trust,* will always take us in a healthy direction.

Polarity in Conversations

Imagine someone is crying and very upset: in that moment they are likely to be in their feminine and need to be heard and listened to. Our immature masculine however, will generally want to fix the problem. This may come from a very loving place, but it's the last thing that the feminine needs. She needs compassion, listening to, and understanding *(compassion is like the emotions of love, joy, and happiness in that it is not gender-specific).* If the immature feminine's sadness is met with the immature masculine, a behavioural pattern will emerge; it will differ depending on the personalities of the two people involved, but generally will lead to a reinforcement of immature behaviours. In these moments, it is much better for the feminine to be met with:

- the mature masculine (as a lover or father figure);
- the mature feminine (as a sister or mother figure);
- the immature feminine (to simply offer sympathy or to encourage and explore their shadows in a healthy or sometimes an unhealthy way);
- avoiding the immature masculine (although this is where most reactive behaviours will take us for as long as we have fear).

When you notice similar dynamics in your life, it's helpful to take out the diagrams and see if you can identify patterns, asking:

- What dynamics are happening?
- What do you and your partner need to do to make them healthy:
  - firstly, within yourself?
  - and then for the other?

When we look at a conversation, polarity and duality are everywhere, as there is a constant moving between our masculine and feminine poles, but it's often hard to notice separation between the masculine and feminine, especially when there is no conflict. *The truth is, we are all whole and integrated people,* the moving between our poles is what creates life and allows time to move forward: by understanding the poles and being able to recognize their separation, we can see how we are each individually integrated and understand each other more.

One reason why women stereotypically don't appear logical is their multi-faceted, multi-dimensional nature: the feminine's expression of diversity is reliant on illogical or emotional behaviour. The paradox of emotions is that once we understand that they are necessary for us to enjoy life, it becomes completely logical for us to have and develop emotions, although from a reductionist perspective these emotions are often illogical. Logic tells us that for something to exist, it needs a real and valid polarity. This means that logic itself *(logic existing within the experience of the separate self),* needs something *illogical* which is valid and essential in nature to exist: this is fulfilled by our emotional and energetic bodies.

As we will discuss later, there are emotions of our mind and there are emotions better described as etheric emotional energy *(often experienced as empathy).* When we talk of the emotional body or emotional intelligence, we are referring to this etheric emotional energy that is all around us, animates us, and generates life force. *Although proven by science, life force energy is hard to define because how it works is always changing, depending on who the observer is,* how they feel, and their preconceptions.

The feminine's purpose is to create life, not to understand it.

In deciding that we understand something, naming it and labelling it on a psychological level, we often stop its evolution. As long as there is un-surety of something, as long as there is a paradox, as long as there are contradicting truths, then the Feminine, in this sense, will always be here building more layers of life and experience: more layers of polarity and duality.

The masculine, primarily the immature masculine, provides us with a more solid, scientific base and understanding. He is always trying to understand life and the universe: which comes with the danger of creating a binary-based, black and white world. To keep the word colourful and joyful, the Masculine needs to have knowledge and understanding of how reality works, knowledge that is greater than himself, the separate self, thus we often look to or create Gods, but if we believe in God or not, what is equally or more important in acquiring knowledge greater than ourselves, is dedicating time to the feminine, our own feminine and that of others. Ensuring excitement, pleasure, and opportunities to trust and surrender to the desires of the feminine and her expression of unfathomable diversity.

Finding Alignment within Our Double Masculine and Feminine Dynamics

We may understand something perfectly as we read it, but when we "need" to apply it, it's not always so easy. When we are reacting from our unhealthy immature and from our subconscious, trauma-fuelled mind, these simple concepts can become almost impossible to apply, especially when trying to communicate with others. We should aim to develop our use of the polarity framework to the point where it is also subconscious, so used without thinking (like driving a car), understanding and integrating the separation and splits within ourselves, even when fearful and in the middle of arguments.

Living multiple truths simultaneously without mental conflict happens when we have alignment. As we will explore later: one of the best places to explore this alignment is through our sexuality. This is where both we, and our partner are more likely to embody our most authentic expressions of masculine and feminine energies, regardless of how aligned they are to our gender. Our physical, mental, and emotional bodies start to find balance with the other's unique energies. This creates inner alignment, not just within the individual, but within the couple during sexual union, and if this level of alignment is maintained outside of sex (which is difficult, but not impossible), arguments are very unlikely. Unhealthy immature double masculine and feminine dynamics do not manifest, neither do moments of joint intellectual disconnect from the masculine, or joint feelings of apathy, loss of drive, and motivation from the feminine.

18
The Immature Fights the Immature

~

When people, stereotypically men, are not given the opportunity to evolve, be it financially, concerning free time, or access to the needed knowledge and wisdom, the immature masculine will often search out and fight another immature masculine. It's hard, almost impossible, for most of us to stay at the same level of development, to simply be content until a mature solution for all, a solution for evolution emerges. We need creative conflict and tension, and if this is not found in a positive way by evolving the immature into the mature, the masculine will often try to push someone else "down" for the *false* feeling that they are going "up". The truth is that their ego feels more powerful in this scenario by creating separation, but this kind of power does not last. Overall, it promotes devolution and the creation of shadows. This egoic, power-over mindset, as opposed to a power-with mindset, is described very well in biology.

There is no hierarchy in the cells of our body, for instance in a eukaryotic cell the most basic and common type there is no hierarchy. Everything is in a mutually dependent relationship. However, if that cell mutates, the mutation of that cell spreads to further mutate other cells and then a power-over system begins in the body, a hierarchy is created. These mutated cells are called cancerous cells. A power-over system in biology creates a mono-culture of sickness and disease that destroys diversity and leads to death. And a power-over system in society and in our culture, does the same.

Throughout history, we can see how the immature masculine has searched for differences as an excuse to engage in power-over behaviour:

- whites against blacks;
- religious wars;
- gang violence;
- football club rivalry;
- political party rivalry;
- North vs. South, East vs. West, this side of the river vs. that side, etc.

Everywhere the immature masculine is looking for differences to create a polarity that reaffirms its own separation. To stop racism, to stop religious wars, to stop terrorism, and the stoning of women, to stop street violence, and the degradation of neighbourhoods, to stop civil wars, the answer is always the same. The individuals involved need the mature feminine to bring them into their mature masculine and they need mature masculine and feminine structures to govern them with individual help and support available, in any such transition. The world needs people who demonstrate and live from these mature principles in positions of power. As we live in a vibrational and reflective universe, the best way to bring something into the world is to *"be it"*, or *"nurture the polarity that supports it"*, as opposed to rejecting it, which brings it here in an unsupportive and problematic way.

The immature feminine fighting the immature feminine is very similar to where the masculine is fighting for resources, from a mindset of lack and fear; the immature feminine is less direct, but still fighting from fear. The immature feminine mainly operates from a place of manipulation, she uses emotions more fluidly than the masculine and can cloud intellect with them. When the immature feminine relates to the immature feminine, there is often a subtler hierarchy of emotional and mental games going on, rooted in passive-aggressive behaviour, very similarly to how the immature feminine manipulates and has power over men and over the masculine.

When we are driven by fear, fear of losing what we emotionally and mentally perceive ourselves to have, or fear of truly accepting ourselves *because self-acceptance risks rejection from others,* we enter into a world built on a power-over mentality, with unhealthy immature traits. But it is always our free will that gives us the power to change.

To move out of power-over mentality and into power-with, we need to be brave enough to choose love and forgiveness.

19
The More You Are, the More You Are

The more feminine you want to be, the more masculine you need to be. The more masculine you want to be, the more feminine you need to be.

If we want to be more in our mature feminine, we need to develop our mature masculine. The feminine can only have as much freedom and space as the masculine can hold space for, that's what he does, he holds space. If we have a weak masculine with weak boundary issues, our feminine cannot feel safe, nor can she take space or express herself.

Many feminine women and masculine men want to spend the majority of their time expressing the traits associated with their gender, especially when together. There is nothing right or wrong with this, it's just what you want, if you want it that way. When out in the world, this will generally be different, with a more fluid flow between the masculine and feminine. When conflicts arise in relationship, we are more likely to switch between our inner masculine and feminine and also our immature and shadow. If we are in a conscious and aware partnership, then when conflict happens, one of us will consciously shift between our mature masculine and feminine poles to bring the other back into mindfulness and out of reactive behaviour. There are so many different ways to be in life, regardless of our sexual orientation or gender: it's important to explore all the mature and immature traits, including the ones that feel less natural to us, as these are likely to hold our greatest potential for growth.

It's good to note here that if we have spent our whole life avoiding our immature masculine or our immature feminine, we might need to spend some time there before we can truly embody the mature, so don't be disheartened if the mature traits don't come straight away.

When a conscious and aware couple use the polarity framework, we will see dynamics such as: the woman purposefully moving into her mature masculine and the man following her lead, thus moving into his mature feminine. In these moments:

- she is giving him a break, letting his subconscious mind relax from its normal way of being, taking an alternative perspective and gaining new insights.

- he is taking time to be in his feminine so that he can develop his own masculine. This is vitally important for many people, even when in a relationship.
- she is showing him what it means to her to be masculine, what she appreciates about his masculinity and what she wants more of. She is modelling back to him his most desirable behaviours, mixed with the best expressions of her masculinity.

You can be the manliest man in the world, but you can't be in your masculine all of the time. We all need to use the other as a mirror if we are to grow, as opposed to becoming trapped in the immature. When two masculine energies are together in a couple they start to take on each other's traits and influence each other. So, a mature masculine man does not want to be with a woman who has a weak masculine, because this will make him weak. And he does not want to purposefully make her masculine weak even if he is intimidated by her, because it is her version of masculinity that will shape his when he moves into his feminine. So, a man is best with a woman who, when in her masculine, can choose to be as strong and mature as he is, but in her own personal and unique, female way.

She can mirror him at his highest masculine potential as she sees it and when she feels it is appropriate. When she moves back into her feminine and he into his masculine, he can start to give back to her what she just modelled for him. This is why it's so important not to lose ourselves in partnership; the lines between manipulation, co-creation, being ourselves and being our partner, can become very thin.

It is really helpful when we can view our relationships as their own conscious entities, because this allows us to detach more easily. Noticing where we previously would have manipulated the other to get our needs met, instead we can see where the relationship meets our needs and where we need to meet our needs elsewhere.

A woman who enjoys being in and living her full feminine nature is *unlikely* to spend too much time expressing her masculinity, she needs to go into her masculine in a very deep and profound way, creating moments of powerfulness that are full of clarity, intent, and have a real impact. A very strong mature masculine, does not need thousands of words, a few simple and respected ones, or a few actions are normally enough. Generally, people acting from their mature masculine will use fewer words and they will be more mindful, but this is not always the case.

Looking at this example the other way around: a woman who tries to keep her man's feminine weak and in the immature will be very unhappy as when she steps into her mature masculine, she is likely to be met with attention-seeking; blaming; manipulation; passive-aggressive behaviour and victimhood. This is the only imprint of the feminine that he has to give her. The self-assurance, empathy, devotion, acceptance, and healing that she needs to receive in order to be all of these things herself, are simply not there. She has not given enough of it to her male partner in order for her to receive it. So, by manipulating men, blaming them, demonstrating overly anxious and emotional behaviour, the feminine stops herself from experiencing her mature feminine.

When we truly realize that everyone in our life is a mirror and understand the Masculine and Feminine Polarity Framework, this knowledge becomes second nature. There are exceptions with this method and no hard and fast rules. Someone who spends a lot of time in their masculine and talks a lot may *not* be weak and operating from their immature, for example, philosophers; politicians; wise teachers; councillors, and academics, all generally need to have a well-developed masculine side to do their job well, although not all operate from their mature masculine, though many do and they still talk a lot.

The art of good conversation from the masculine is being able to tap into the feminine frequently, leaving very few dead ends or ultimatums. Perhaps one reason more feminine people like to talk so much, is because in doing it well, they glimpse the endless possibilities and potentials of life.

A common example of an unbalanced masculine and feminine is:

"I want to be more in my feminine, but I lack clarity" (clarity being more masculine).
or
"I want to be in my masculine, but I don't have enough self-assurance and confidence" (self-assurance and confidence being more feminine).

In both of these cases, what the person needs is more of the other to become who and what they want to be.

If we want to have a healthy mature masculine, we need to develop our feminine, *thus masculine men and people with a strong immature masculine should focus on those traits labelled to be more feminine on the polarity framework:*

- Be self-assured. Don't let doubts, fears, or judgements enter our mind. Self-assurance supports us to act with discernment in a humble way.
- Welcome diversity. The masculine needs a level of diversity to sustain himself, and diversity will always foster interdependent relationships. He needs potential confusion to demonstrate his masculine principles. The immature rejects diversity and interdependence because he fears losing control.
- Be empathic. Have empathy for people acting in their immature. This helps them to evolve and self-realize, and supports us to honour them instead of shaming and judging.
- Be devoted to the masculine principle. Show full commitment and dedication to the path of masculinity itself, penetrating truth to hold an infinite and timeless knowing of the universe. Never give up on yourself and work for the outer manifestation of your femininity that you wish to worship and adore.
- Have compassion, celebrating others and feeling joy, for their joy enables us to be more generous with our love, because we feel more love.
- Be intuitive. Without intuition, we are cut off from our higher selves. We then only know what our conscious mind knows and this leads us back to the immature. Mature masculine people need to live with emotional and mental balance, but always being able follow their intuition when it arises.
- Accept most things, even when you don't want to. After you accept it, either the feminine will transform it, or you will move into your masculine and have the power to change reality through action. Selfless, egoless actions that serve the whole, are always more powerful.
- Be creative and be auspicious. The feminine attracts her desires like a magnet; she is auspicious by nature. The masculine turns his desires into goals, and then he aims for them: he walks the path to the goal he sets, and is rewarded with the fulfilment of his desire when he gets there. But we are both masculine and feminine, so do both, be wise and discerning and use the law of attraction to help you hit your targets and reach your goals.
- Express freedom and trust and you will remember why it's important to hold the boundaries that protect it.
- Heal the immature masculine to allow more mindfulness into the world.

And to be more feminine, we need to act from our mature masculine, thus feminine women and people with a strong immature feminine, should focus on these *traits labelled to be more masculine on the polarity framework:*

- Be humble, know when you deserve respect and allow it to come to you naturally. This will increase your self-assurance.
- Acknowledge and act from interdependence, because independence is a lie (no one can be truly independent, we all need others and love from others at some point in our lives) and dependence is a prison. Interdependent actions allow diversity to flourish.
- Honour ourselves, others, and all of creation. If we find it hard to honour another, especially when we disagree with them, we can honour all that they are learning through their mistakes. We honour the journey and have empathy for the pain that will shape them.
- Worship the divine feminine in all things, even the masculine, allowing the masculine to be devoted to you.
- Be magnanimous, generous and kind, as this supports us in feeling joy for another's joy.
- Strive for emotional and mental balance. When we are not able to act from our intuition, we need to strive for emotional and mental balance, as when we do this our intuition becomes readily available.
- Be selfless. Act for the expansion of selflessness, the realization of non-separation, interconnectedness, and the greater whole where all power and creativity comes from.
- Apply wisdom and mental concepts from different places in a way that serves the greater whole to experience more freedom, trust, and creativity.
- Responsibility, holding space, and boundaries. Take responsibility for everything in reality, acknowledge that we are the creators of our universe. The more of reality the masculine encompasses, the more space he holds for the feminine, giving her freedom to express life, to express femininity. But holding this space requires strong boundaries, strong Yes's and No's. The difficulty lies in knowing when and how to move our boundaries to change our yes, and change our no, without the collapse of what we hold.
- Be mindful. When we are mindful, we are in our healthy ego. Reactive behaviours of the unhealthy ego cannot exist in mindfulness, so we can heal.

And when using the polarity framework as our guiding mental concept, in both the masculine and feminine we need to:

- Love conditionally and for as much as our capacity allows, unconditionally.
- Have sex consciously with mindfulness, in a way that heals. We can still follow our animalistic urges and have hard rough sex—to say that any of this is bad is a judgement. As long as we are learning and growing from our experiences, we should allow ourselves the freedom to do as we wish. Providing we have the consent of our partner, this can even be to dominate or to be submissive if this is our truth at the time. But ideally, we will progress to conscious sex, sex that evolves the masculine and feminine, not sex that creates greater shadow.

The qualities that we attribute to masculine and feminine are not black and white. We can still be controlling and in our feminine, or we can be manipulative in our masculine. The qualities and traits are typical of that expression, but we can be in any expression and demonstrate any quality at any time: the chances are, that the more we demonstrate it, the more likely we are to move into and stay in the masculine or feminine energy that best represents it.

It's important not to get too wrapped up in words or labels, acknowledging that from one perspective we are always our integrated self, having this experience of polarity so that we can have greater understanding of ourselves with more depth and more complexity in a very beautiful and simplistic way. The purpose of this is not to become one another, we live in duality and separation for a reason; it's how we learn. And polarity (sometimes experienced as conflict) is what pushes our evolution forward, but ultimately oneness is truth and thus we are most attracted to the people whose inner masculine or feminine matches our own.

Romantically and paradoxically, we are all looking for our perfect match: our polar opposite, who is similar to us.

Part 2

SEX AND OTHER APPLICATIONS OF THE POLARITY FRAMEWORK

....

Note

As this book is intended to reach a mainstream audience, many chapters on sex and sexuality have been taken out and published on social media and elsewhere. It feels important to give an insight into sex and our sexuality from the polarity and duality, masculine and feminine, perspective so some of the major and most helpful aspects are covered here.

Please note, when looking at how etheric and sexual energy relates to the human energy centres, there can only be guidelines, as we all have free will and the power to manipulate and change how energy flows. The following chapters look at common and natural pathways and it is better to understand, develop and experience these before developing a personal practice and exerting will-power as many Tantric Teachings suggest.

....

20
Sex

~

When a man orgasms and does not ejaculate, his energy stays in his masculine: determined, focused and powerful. But if he ejaculates, his energy will most likely switch into his feminine; the drive goes, the feeling that he can knock down walls with his fists subsides, the man becomes softer and depending on his mood—this can be enjoyable and pleasurable—he might feel inspired, creative and intuitive, or if he needs a lot of inner healing and integration, he might just want to sleep.

The woman's polarity is also likely to switch from being receptive and in a place of surrender, to being focused, with a sense of strength and power: which may not have been her original desire. She will interpret the masculine energy in that moment as we all do, in her own unique way: maybe she starts planning tomorrow, her holiday or some other event, maybe she lays in silence and enjoys the shift in her energy, her polarity just feeling it all in her body with no judgment of masculine or feminine. She might become needy, feeling like she needs something or someone to focus her energy and love into, so turns back to the man with a desire akin to worship. A common image is of the man rolling over to sleep, while the woman lays in bed, feeling energized and staring at the ceiling for a few hours.

When a woman orgasms, her energy comes more into herself, so she moves further into the feminine, surrendering and softening even more.

For a man to move back into his masculine, it really helps when the woman he has just been intimate with orgasms, releasing his power and allowing their polarities to shift back. But for many women, the problem is they feel unable to do this if their sense of masculinity feels more dominant and powerful than the man's. The subconscious fear is that the act of switching polarities in that moment, runs the risk of decreasing both of their potentials instead of increasing them: this perspective is mostly governed by our beliefs, which can change, but generally not overnight. Unfortunately, for many this means that the man needs to go into the stresses of life, taking on pain and suffering until the woman feels that he is strong enough for her to surrender to again. But if the man always ejaculates and the woman does not, then this cycle of stress before sex will be their cycle throughout the partnership or marriage. Thus, for the man sex becomes stress-relief, often leaving the women disappointed. This cultural trend has definitely been changing over recent years, but it is still a truth for many.

When a man orgasms, but does not ejaculate he is able to stay in his power, which allows the woman to surrender more. *And when a woman orgasms and the man does not orgasm or ejaculate,* the same happens. *When a woman orgasms and the man ejaculates with an orgasm,* this brings them closer to a sense of oneness, offering a feeling of spiritual fulfilment. This can be healthy, as long as both parties have enough differences between themselves *(the kind of differences that attract each other),* and a strong sense of individualization and a healthy ego. Unless the aim is to transcend the physical plane, our ego is important as are our differences. This connection between two people (straight or gay) is energetic, so it's not reliant on physical penetration or even being in the same room or country.

Many men (and less women) often unconsciously give their energy away into pornography and fantasy, moving them into their immature and shadow traits. While some women (and less men) are able to trust and surrender to others, which supports them (men and woman) to move back into their healthy mature masculine. For men who never or rarely ejaculate, they can create a lot of power and energy, often more than they know what to do with. For these men, it's important to learn other ways to move into and access their feminine. Just as it's important for women with such men, to learn how to move into their masculine. Our sexuality is key to working with polarity, even if we are choosing to be single or celibate. How this most fundamental dynamic plays out in each of us can be so unique.

- Masculine men should generally beware of women who move them into their feminine and offer no support to move them back into their masculine, as this reduces a person's energy and their level of conscious awareness.
- Feminine women should generally beware of men who both stop them from experiencing their masculinity or always put them into it.

The more aware and mindful we become of how our sexuality moves between our inner polarities, the more we can use this energy within ourselves through self-pleasuring and acts of self-love. It is great to do this with another person, a partner, but learning to use our sexual energy to dive into our own mature feminine's creativity and then back to our own mature masculine's purpose-driven nature, in order to see our inspiration manifest in the world through action and through the use of sexual energy is such a gift.

I'd encourage you to explore and notice the subtle changes in your inner world after sexual activity, with yourself and/or with others, and then see how you can build on these subtle differences to better understand your personal polarity and how you evolve and develop it. There are no right answers when working with polarity in this way and we are free to programme our minds as and how we wish, but the universal laws of polarity and duality will always be working to pull us back into balance.

It is also very important for men to learn how to orgasm in their feminine, to feel the orgasm take them more into themselves and for women to orgasm in their masculine, feeling this gifting of their power and energy to another. Just as this chapter is relevant to gay and lesbian couples, when learning to orgasm in, with and for the traits not associated with our gender: we need to mentally and energetically embody the masculine or feminine energy that opposes our physical gender.

Understanding how masculine and feminine energies flow in our physical bodies helps us achieve this embodiment and a sexual experience with ourselves. Related resources and practices from many different sources can be found online, and if searching the internet is not fruitful you could start by looking at kundalinibodywork.com.

21
Ejaculation and Energy

This is a very deep and important subject with differences in both the masculine and feminine energies, and the male and female bodies in relation to how energy moves and the effects of it. Holistic growth is priority and our cultivation of internal energy and power should be in relation to our overall growth and development, so to teach *"too much"* on non-ejaculation practices through a book, is irresponsible.

Non-ejaculation for men starts to happen naturally without a need to apply "overly forceful retention practices" when we develop our healthy, mature and integrated selves: creating a clear connection between our heart, mind, and sex. When learning to practise non-ejaculation, being able to relate from the heart is the foundation of a successful practice.

A general understanding of this topic is helpful, recognizing the dangerous and irresponsible teachings of some (but not all) Western Tantra teachers and "sexperts" who are putting male non-ejaculation practices before holistic growth and development. Other institutions and movements are promoting abstinence from orgasm and pleasure, stopping the flow of life force completely. Neither of these are beneficial in the long term. Taoist practices are the most helpful, simply suggesting that the older men get, the less they should ejaculate and this is good advice to follow. The number one priority for a man embarking on the non-ejaculation journey, should be to heal your inner feminine, thus developing a good relationship with your heart: if you do this, the rest will follow naturally. Traditional Taoist practices are in line with this statement. Some of the following chapters explore male and female ejaculatory and non-ejaculatory orgasms in more depth and in relation to Masculine and Feminine Polarity Work.

22
Gender, Domination, and Submission

There are no rules, only guidelines. We create our reality, so if our experience is different to the status quo, we should follow and see where it leads and what it has to teach us. But if we change our reality so much that our personal relationship to polarity and duality: to family; society; sexuality; or gender becomes unhelpful, then we can take a few steps back by reframing our situation on the polarity framework. This is particularly relevant to people who struggle with gender identity, or have spent far too long over-identifying as a dominant masculine; a submissive feminine, or any other variation.

It's not to say that any of these choices are necessarily wrong for a person, but the inner integrations of masculine and feminine polarities that create these desires are less common, so the Universe gives us less people to mirror or inspire us with their models of internal polarity, making it harder for us to see when and where we come out of alignment with ourselves and in relation to the collective consciousness: as these two are always in relation.

Our aim should be to follow the guidance of our soul and our higher self in a healthy and integrated way, which in turn will always support the collective. Coming back to a natural expression of masculinity and femininity, regardless of any gender choice or sexual desires, will help us find our personal alignment, inner power, and freedom. We might have tendencies to be a certain way through our DNA, our upbringing, religion, or even astrology, if that's what we believe, but we always have free will and the choice to change, regardless if our choice is to become more or less radical.

If our own inner truth has been polluted with mixed up ideas about gender, being confused if we are predominately masculine or feminine and has turned our *emotional and personality traits* into about being a man or a woman, a girl or a boy, because this is what we were taught, then our inner alignment between our physical, mental, and emotional bodies will often be twisted and harder to find.

Using Masculine and Feminine Polarity Work in this way, helps us find the reset button to explore our relationships with sex, partners, parents and life in a new way. The best way to create this reset is to explore where our polarity gives us sexual pleasure, but without the dogma of being a man or a woman, just simply using traits described as masculine and feminine, noticing we might find a lot of pleasure in the unhealthy and shadow areas of the framework and knowing we can find a lot more once we make these healthy.

For some people, a gender reassignment might be the best choice, but for most, finding their aligned and authentic expression as an individual, within their masculinity and femininity, regardless of gender, will be far more liberating and rewarding, for what that person's higher self is trying to learn and experience in this lifetime. And for nearly all people, finding balance between being dominant and submissive and in our immature and mature expressions and desires, will always be a far healthier way to live, opposed to being overly identified or stuck in any one mode of being.

The Desire to Win and Lose in Sex Is the Same

As a man comes close to orgasm every woman, including the woman he's with, becomes a Goddess. In Hinduism the Goddess Lalita represents the *maya*, the illusion, a woman of a thousand and eight faces. If the man ejaculates into her, cums into her, he comes deeper into the illusion, maya, her reality. The spending of his seed in the reflection of himself creates more life, creates more self. As a Goddess she desires this, she desires his life, his seed, to create more life so her maya and reality continue. But she also desires a God, a man who can love and desire her but not be seduced by her and lose his freewill and control. She wants a man who can hold her with so much presence and awareness that he lifts her out of her own illusion. The physical manifestation of this is holding his Lingham in her Yoni while she orgasms without spilling his seed.

We all want the illusion of life and separation to continue, because oneness wants to know itself, but we also want to break free, to understand our illusion and know truth. By knowing the truth and while still being in the illusion we are able to take a step back and create life from conscious awareness, the purity of our conscious awareness. Many would say this is the essence of Tantra and Advaita, to be awake and conscious of our illusion in order to shape it.

From our immature perspective (which is still a truth and should not be denied) we want to dominate the illusion and others, and to be submissive to the illusion and others. Both are always true, our desire to be dominant and submissive, to know we are God and to feel God guiding our life. When we live in duality with a sense of fear and from our immature self, we are generally forced into being dominant or submissive. To control or be controlled. Once our understanding deepens and our fear is removed, we can see all four desires are within us, and within others. The desire:

- to be dominant;
- to be submissive;
- to worship the feminine;
- to be devoted to the masculine.

Every action is depicted by where our focus is, and just because our focus is on one of these four parts it does not take our capacity away for the other three or make them untrue. A key to life is recognizing when we play one of these parts, we must be projecting (attracting or resisting) the others outside of ourselves. It is our projections that dictate our experience and our reality.

When we no longer reject ourself, not even our immature and shadow parts, then we start to create a world we truly love. One where it is okay to fully play with and explore all our sides, living in the present but not lost in momentary illusion, overly identifying with being masculine or feminine, dominant or submissive.

The answer is always changing but for most of us it lies in trusting ourself enough so we find people in our life, men and women, who we trust enough to follow, and from the perspective of our immature: trust enough to submit to. And just as importantly we need to trust ourselves enough so that we can give this same gift to others. And for some of us it is simply about expanding conscious awareness beyond duality, beyond a truth that can be written.

Why We Want What We Cannot Have . . . and How to Have It!

For men or the masculine principle, the desire is to be so attracted to the feminine, to beauty and to life, that all we can do is surrender. Surrender our seed for her children, our money for her life, and our time for her happiness. Sex sells because many men, and the immature masculine, want to be seduced. But when the masculine surrenders in this way he dies the proverbial death, the poles change at the point of peak orgasm and the

109

man becomes feminine, and the woman masculine. Rarely are either truly happy in this moment; these orgasms release chemicals in the brain that give us temporary happiness but deep down both parties know that sex should not end like this, it should not end in peak orgasm followed by unconsciousness. If men and women are to evolve, then sex needs to evolve. The reason why so many men become addicted to porn or choose to give their money to beautiful women who seduce them, is because they crave escape, they do not understand duality well enough to harness and use their power so they surrender it to the feminine who takes their energy and transmutes it as she chooses.

Many men are unconscious to what's going on, they don't understand how they lost their power and they want it back, and many are even oblivious to the power they had in the first place or what it is. They spend most of their time going through life asleep, with a low level of consciousness and a dense vibration.

The feminine wants to stay in her feminine, she likes, loves and enjoys her Shakti nature, but she also wants to sublimate the man's energy, his power. In one hand she wants to metaphorically kill him, taking his power and ridding the world of weakness, to take the Sun from his eyes and give him a son or a daughter (moon). Great sexual excitement comes from these often unconscious primordial survival beliefs and programmes. And on the other hand she wants him to be a source of unlimited power and love, one which she can always draw from. The sun that shines on the moon and reflects life.

To change, we need to become more honest with ourselves, understand what drives our sexual desires and when and where we need to apply resistance. Sex needs to be fun so how we apply resistance might keep changing but men and the masculine in all of us need to learn how to hold power and sexual seed during orgasm, and women and the feminine in all of us need to learn how not to pull it, how not to kill every man taken to bed, and how to transmute and sublimate sexual energy.

23

The Power I Feel When
I Do Something Bad

For some people, some of the time, they believe that when they do something bad, they create a kind of inner power. But as we are learning, good and bad are judgments created by the mind: this power was there the whole time. It's the mind saying:

"Now I can allow myself this power because . . ."
or
"Now I have more or less power because . . ."

That creates the self-belief that generates the power. In part, it is healthy that the mind restricts the amount of power we allow ourselves because, an occasional sense of lack and more often a sense of power, is helpful for us in that we construct a reality with a form of balance.

But when the mind is unintegrated with the body, our emotions and higher self, we create our experience of power from a power-over level of awareness, thus doing bad things and having power-over someone gives us more power. They feel less power, so therefore we must have more, or we have a secret something that they don't know about, so our mind allows us to feel power.

People demonstrate this behaviour in relatively petty things, like shop lifting, also known as kleptomania (not to say that shop lifting is okay), which also gives a boost of adrenalin to support the feeling of power generated. Some people do mildly mean and secretive things to the people that they love, like giving them too much sugar on purpose, slowly turning off their immune system. The feeling of taking something from someone else, or stopping them from doing something, is creating the dualistic belief that they have less, so I must have more. Similarly, our economy is built on a system of power-over, and as much as we try to change it on the outside, what we really need to change is on the inside:

- our behaviours;
- our value systems;
- our trust in life;
- and our trust in each other and a higher purpose

If we do not change this, then our understanding of life and our approach to money, will always be stuck in a power-over perspective, compared to a power-with perspective: so, on the largest scale, the economy will never change and more suffering will be in the collective consciousness than is helpful.

Power can be an addiction and for people susceptible to this kind of addiction, for whatever reason, if they are not careful it can lead them to committing bigger crimes or developing violent tendencies, so for these people it's even more urgent that they grasp the concept and feel the joys and pleasures of a power-with existence. Taking power away and punishing people who commit crimes and violent acts only perpetuates power-over thinking, so will only create more crime and violence.

People in prisons need rehabilitation: they need shadow work, they need to develop their inner Feminine so that they can forgive, love, accept themselves, and accept others. And even more controversially, they need to include their sexuality, to help them find and heal their inner feminine. It's very difficult to heal mentally or emotionally without including our sexuality because, nearly everything in life is connected to sex.

Without developing the mature feminine during rehabilitation, it's very difficult to embody mature masculine traits, which are exactly what prisons and other institutions, for the most part should be achieving: releasing people back into society who take responsibility for their actions; can control emotional outbursts; be humble; be selfless and hold space for others to demonstrate their mature masculine and feminine traits.

24
The Empath and the Narcissist

"Inside every narcissist, there is a suppressed empath, and in every empath, a narcissist, forced to balance life through ill behaviour."

In relationships where one person sees themselves as an empath and the other as a narcissist, there is often deep, unconscious and unresolved guilt and shame in the partner who identifies as an empath.

Using the laws of polarity and duality to understand life, we can see that some narcissists really do love and accept "themselves" completely, but most accept what they love about their ego and project what they do not onto others, or opt into total denial. The work for most people who show strong narcissistic traits is developing mature masculine qualities such as interdependence, co-operation, and selflessness: selflessness in relation to seeing beyond individuality and living from a sense of knowledge and oneness.

An empath dating a narcissist, who is not working on themselves in a healthy and balanced way, for example with shadow work, is very likely to make the narcissist more narcissistic. Laws of polarity and duality, and attraction and resistance teach us that we are most attracted to people who are a good representation of our own inner masculine and feminine dynamics, good mirrors, our perfect opposite. But because most of us do not judge ourselves as "perfect", and because our own integration of the different polarities and dualities that make us up often have a lot of unhealthy immature characteristics in them, then it means that our "perfect" partner, is often "bad" for us. If we are more empathic and we fall in love with someone who is more narcissistic, and we end up hating them later, it would be wise for us to look into the unhealthy, immature quadrants and shadows of the polarity framework to help us identify where we need to change, instead of blaming the other, blaming our reflection. Because most empathic people identify with being nice, loving, and caring, where they reject their shadow, their partner balances it out and in the empath's case, massively amplifies it. The more an empath has deep hidden guilt and shame, then the more the narcissist will display "negative" behaviours to balance out the emotions that the other is not able to accept internally.

Unfortunately, most empaths will disagree and say that they "have done their shadow work and have very little guilt or shame left". Consciously this is most likely true, but if we look deeper into the unconscious mind, most of us will find a different truth. Western society is narcissistic to the core, it is self-centred, ego driven, and materialistic. It is the pinnacle of the immature masculine and feminine combined. Unhealthy competitiveness with a strong victim mentality: creating victims for financial success, or protecting victims in courts with legal proceedings, we are a society that is dependent on and supports an unhealthy victim mentality. Deep down in the West we all know that our life is still being built on the suffering of people in poorer countries, it is getting better in some cases, but unconscious guilt and shame is still heavy in our collective.

Many (but not all) positive affirmations and abundance practices, teach us to ignore and deny this if we want success, their logic is: "If good people focus on the good in themselves, then the world will become a reflection of this goodness, positivity breeds positivity, so it really is okay to ignore blood diamonds, the arms trade, living and working conditions of people growing our food, sweat shops, child labour." This list goes on, but I'll stop here as I think you'll benefit if you read to the end of this book. The approach of personal transformation before planetary has merit and is where we should start, but we have to work on the global too, which includes our unconscious guilt and shame for it, by correcting it. And believe it or not, doing this will reduce the number of narcissists and narcissistic behaviour in our world.

To check if you feel guilt and shame around these issues, see if defensive thoughts came into your mind as you read this, or if you completely dissociated from the text, reading but not taking a word in. Responses such as "yes but I . . .", or "I give so much of my time to . . .", "my money to . . .", means the mind is becoming defensive and is likely trying to hide from unconscious guilt and shame. So, to heal narcissistic behaviour in our partner, or to attract a partner who will not abuse us in this way, first we need to accept the guilt and/or shame for being privileged, for living in a society where we don't suffer so much, but others do: we can only heal this by changing it, and the first step to changing something is accepting it.

Personal shadow work, sexual and non-sexual, is so important to stop us pushing someone else into the role of being bad, because we are attached to being loving and kind. Both collective shadow work (understanding the shadow of humanity) and embodying the mature masculine principle (taking responsibility for the shadow of humanity), are essential to healing our subconscious guilt and shame which for the most part is simply inherited by being born privileged. Narcissists and empaths are not by default more masculine or feminine, they are both integrated mixes and better viewed as archetypes than traits, but understanding the Masculine and Feminine Polarity Framework and shadow work, is a great tool to heal this dynamic.

25
Importance of Worship and Honouring

The more the masculine worships the feminine, the more the feminine can honour and be devoted to the masculine, and the more the feminine honours and is devoted to the masculine, the more the masculine can worship the feminine.

Ultimately, this relationship is within ourselves and fundamental to our growth and development, but it is okay to want and have a relationship of worship and honouring on the outside too if it makes our lives more fun, sexy, pleasurable, and worth living.

The spiritual purpose of worship has been severely skewed over the years: if you look into some aspects of Hinduism, such as tantra, a higher purpose in ceremonial and worshipping practices is still clear, especially around sexuality, but many modern-day spiritual practices, in both the East and West, are missing the point. People are lost in preforming actions and rituals from their mind, experiencing separation from what they are worshipping instead of recognizing their interconnectedness to it.

A similar situation is true in how we honour and respect others and institutions in society. Honour and respect are often forced onto us as a means of survival, indoctrination, and control or for us to get what we want. True honouring that comes from our heart, is both given and received in a very different way with different results. Gaia, Mother Earth, Planet Earth, Pachamama, or whatever name works for us, has been both honoured and worshipped by many cultures and religions throughout history. While Gaia sustains life on earth, she has also been the most destructive force known to man, up until the atom bomb.

The awesome force of both Gaia and the atom bomb, deserve a certain level of respect. Similarly, many religious Gods and Goddesses are depicted as both magnanimous and cruel, lifting us to heaven or sentencing us to eternal damnation. Both of these examples depict a higher power that we are at the mercy of, with our own death and destruction being a likely outcome. But for some reason, people still desire, although manipulated at times, to worship these higher powers that cause their own death, destruction, and eternal damnation.

Some people, with no religious connotations at all, find so much sexual excitement from another having power and control over their life, that they literally give their power away in fantasy and reality so they can experience the rush of emotion that comes from surrender, generating feelings of unconditional love through various acts. Thus, higher truths are misunderstood and the desire to give and receive unconditional love can lead us into taking dangerous and twisted actions.

Un-programming and de-conditioning a lifetime of false beliefs, fears, and societal conditioning, is not always easy. Forgiving ourselves is important, but so is not losing the deeper meaning of what led us to the actions that we now regret and need to forgive—in England, we say don't throw the baby out with the bath water. The more we love, forgive, and learn to love unconditionally, the more access we have to our power: life really is this simple from a meta perspective. But having the power to turn light into dark or heaven into hell because we got angry, or our feeling of love momentarily turned into hate, is a scary feat, thus an elite number try to control the masses but unfortunately, a large number of this elite are governed from their egos' desires, not their souls or a connection to God. To get ready for a world where it really is the free will of humanity running the show and not the egoic power of a few individuals, we need to learn to both:

- listen to our soul and its desires;
- to make the desires of our ego healthy, ensuring balance in this dynamic.

When we look at honouring—the honouring of a higher power or the masculine—there is a desire for direction and leadership. This act of honouring gives us freedom through surrender and the more we trust into something greater than ourselves, the freer we feel. From our immature, this can become very disempowering: God has a plan, so I don't need one. Or this holy book or scripture will lead me to liberation, so I do not need to liberate myself with my own discernment and my own knowing. An act like this is a total rejection of our mature self and the deeper meaning of most religious teachings and teachers such as Jesus. We end up blocking our evolution by interpreting religious texts, fables, and scriptures incorrectly. They are here to help guide us to our own healthy conclusions: a path towards greater connection, community, and an understanding of our individual power, use of free will and oneness.

Freedom through surrender is true, not just in religion, but also in psychology, it's why some people love the relationship that they have with their sensei in a martial arts gym, or the structure of the church, or military, and why some become fanatical about a football team or a pop star. Their happiness is no longer in their hands, they have given it to a higher power. It does not matter so much if we give it to God or a football team. By finding it hard to compare ourselves to this higher power, we find it easier to be in a place of surrender and to experience the feminine. Whether they win or lose the football match, some happiness is gained through the act of surrendering our happiness and joy to this higher power. The pleasure comes from being able to trust in our chosen team and unconscious pleasure, and even comes from forgiving them when they lose, as this is a true demonstration of our love and commitment.

Worship allows us to experience the feeling of unconditional love before we have truly learned to love ourselves and others unconditionally. Through the practice of worship and white tantra (white tantra in part being devotional through mantra, prayer and meditation), we do not judge ourselves so harshly because the act of worship puts us into a place of unconditional giving of unconditional love; giving in this way opens the heart. It is why some people feel good after religious worship and continue to do it: when we give in this way, our heart truly opens so the act of giving love is akin to receiving love.

If we are not religious, don't like ceremonies, football, or idolizing celebrities then we might choose to experience unconditional love, trust, and surrender, through worshipping and honouring our lover, husband, or wife. Wanting to be worshipped or honoured can easily bring us into our unhealthy immature, so we must really evolve and develop as an individual so that we can allow our partner(s) to have these experiences of worship and honouring, of unconditional love, trust, and surrender in a healthy way that does not bring either party into their unhealthy aspects or develop shadow traits in a negative way. Remembering that allowing our partner or lover to love us in this way, opens their heart and by allowing them to give to us unconditionally, we are giving them the greatest gift. When we can worship a God, a Goddess, Gaia, our lover, wife, or husband knowing that ultimately, we are a reflection of them, every act of worship becomes an act of self-love.

For some people, the idea of role-playing with such scenarios can be blasphemous. For others, it's dangerous, twisting the higher truths into self-serving ego and power trips, so we have to be careful. One of the best ways to make sure that we do not fall into our immature, is to start honouring and worshipping ourselves and learning to use the concepts of inner masculine and feminine, mature and immature, healthy and unhealthy, and the shadow.

As religions start to take a back seat, becoming less relevant in people's lives, we should not lose the powerful and somewhat hard to grasp lessons that they can teach us about concepts such as worship and honouring, but also about the mystical parts of life that we each have the ability for, be it Yogis levitating, siddhis of clairvoyance, or Jesus healing the sick and turning water into wine.

God is within the hearts of us all.

26
Surrender, Trust, Power, and Forgiveness
~

In this chapter, we start to apply the polarity framework in a more fluid way, exploring the relationships between "surrender and power" and "trust and forgiveness", and how the two tie into one another without explicitly putting these traits onto the polarity framework. Notice that there is no exact right answer as to what is masculine or feminine, immature or mature; this is often down to our individual perspective and way of seeing the world that can change with each situation.

By exercising our mind to think in polarity and duality, we will start to unconsciously apply the framework in a paradoxical way as it is intended.

Surrendering to Orgasm

When we look at what happens in sex between a man and a woman, and for ease of the examples, the man being in his masculine and the woman being in her feminine, the woman will have the desire to surrender to the masculine and in doing so, she allows his energy to transform her. When the "man" releases his sperm and/or energy into the woman, it becomes a part of her and she has no other choice in that moment but to take it, to surrender to it, allowing the energy it contains to become a part of her.

Unfortunately, if the man has not been taking good care of himself, then he will have released a lot of negativity into the woman: all of his recent experiences are translated into an energy and a vibration that is stored in his sperm, that he has now released into her. This process, is the same in non-ejaculatory and lesbian sex, but to a lesser degree. Some men find this hard to believe, but many women are sensitive enough to confirm it, so if you are unsure, ask a few friends.

If the man has been taking care of himself, then the feminine partner will be much more receptive to his energy, and it will be easier for her to work with it: to increase life force and to manifest (attract into their lives what she desires).

In the first scenario, where the masculine energy is polluted with violence, pornography, and other negative qualities, it can be hard for the feminine to transform this energy once inside of her and she can be consumed by it.

120

Her vibration is likely to lower to match the energy that has just been put inside of her, as it overpowers her stability and higher vibrations. She starts to live and act from her immature in an unhealthy way, but often unconscious of what's happening.

If the sex was enjoyable, then the lower vibrational energies in the immature and shadow can feel enjoyable too, so from the subconscious mind, we might start to crave and desire more of what is not *"good"* for us. To stop this from happening, the feminine partner needs to keep her vibrations high, so that she can transmute the darkest of energies. To do this in her daily life, she must focus on being a whole person, *not just a half,* her mature masculine needs to be strong, to hold space, and offer wisdom, humility, selflessness, discernment, mindfulness, and emotional and intellectual balance, because it is these mature masculine qualities that support her to stay in her mature feminine. Without them within herself and within her partner, she is likely to slip into the immature, being consumed by darkness and negativity. The feminine pole is designed to transmute darkness and negativity through love, forgiveness, and acceptance and through this act, her masculine counterpart becomes *more* mature.

When the feminine can raise her vibration to a place of love and acceptance of the negative energy that the man, the outer masculine force, has just given her, then it cannot stick. We have to be a vibrational match for negative energy to stay with us. Although, if we are exposed to enough negative energy for long enough, then it's likely that our vibration will lower, but this is true in all of life. When our vibration is high, negative energy will simply transform into raw primal energy that we use with our free will and this relates to how Kundalini energy works in the body, because Kundalini is generated by the polarity of masculine and feminine energies within and without.

We all need to learn how to transmute negative energy, the energy within ourselves, our partners, and the energies that we pick up in daily life, not just through sex but through commuting to work, grocery shopping, watching TV, and any and all other activities that are not meditation. Transmuting negative energy, being loving, accepting, and forgiving is not just the job of women, but the job of the feminine that exists in us all, so it is also important for men to learn how to run and transmute energy through their feminine pathways.

Energy is amplified in sex, so the polarities become easier to see, but both men and women, the masculine and feminine, are transforming and transmuting energy during sex. It does not make sense to try and find balance and equality here as it involves too many judgements and brings us into the mind, it's better to understand that the feminine partner's role is to take more and transform more and the masculine partner's role is to give more: *and it's only when the feminine partner does her job well, that the masculine receives transformed energy back, otherwise he just loses out.*

In a more ideal situation, we see a feminine partner *within us and without,* who can use creativity and is guided by intuition. She is able to dance with masculine energy, the positivity and negativity in both her masculine and feminine poles, and the poles of others while feeling safe enough to surrender. Whether surrendering to the masculine within herself (through self-pleasuring), or without of herself, during sex, and other intimate interactions, she is saying yes to all of him without necessarily understanding or agreeing with him, saying yes to his light and his dark, and in doing this, he feels completely accepted, so his energy is able to raise and transform.

If during sexual intercourse he ejaculates into her and she orgasms, then he too is surrendering and she has little choice but to surrender them both to the feminine, to her intuition, and their higher selves. His egoic, earthly, masculine power is too weak in that moment to hold her. As discussed in the opening chapter of this section, *if he orgasms and does not ejaculate, then he can stay in his masculine power and continue to hold space for her, and if he ejaculates but she does not orgasm, then he will move into his feminine and she will move into her masculine.*

There is nothing wrong with the man moving into the feminine pole and the woman into the masculine at the end of sex: life is about experiencing both through one gender. The feminine has the choice to keep more control over the energy that the masculine just released into her, turning it into whatever she chooses: *life is created by the feminine from masculine energy. To create life, to create a child, the masculine needs to surrender his seed and move into his feminine.* Sexual energy is raw potential life force, we can make children from it, heal our bodies with it, or use the energy on the mental level to manifest our own and our loved one's dreams.

When a mature, sexually conscious man and woman are engaged in sexual activity, then it's possible for them to learn to circulate and increase their energy, allowing conscious awareness to spread until they feel a sense of merger with each other, themselves, and God: while also acknowledging their sense of separation and seeing it as the gift that it is. The more conscious, aware, and evolved the couple are, the longer that they can sustain this feeling of bliss.

A deeper look into ancient Eastern sexual practices, starts to reveal ways of doing this, but first it's important to purify the mind and the body. It's why some teachers insist on Yoga and other practices and disciplines for years before teaching this knowledge, and why I support people to emotionally detox to understand their masculine and feminine energies and dynamics through the polarity framework, and to develop an open heart before teaching sexual arts in workshops. The Taoist teacher, Mantak Chia, is another great resource for physical practices in this, and Osho, who was largely responsible for bringing Tantra to the West, is another great alternative resource.

Masculine partners need to learn how to . . .

. . . intuitively listen to their feminine partner so, after verbal consent they only give her energy when all of her bodies are open and receptive: the physical, mental, emotional, and spiritual and then they need to learn (although not essential, as we can still be happy without) to have non-ejaculatory orgasms, so that their physical power is not wasted and the level of depth in their connection and in sexual union is greater. From here, new depths are added to the masculine and feminine surrender dynamic, but before moving into these advanced sexual practices, it is important that we have evolved personally with relatively healthy, integrated, and balanced mature (and immature) masculine and feminine states: which for the masculine, is the process of embodying our inner feminine to evolve the masculine. We need to understand what happens to a woman when we release our energy into her and we need to learn to care; to clean ourselves from too much negativity and toxicity so that when she desires to surrender, we are able to allow her.

And feminine partners need to learn . . .

. . . to say no when they don't want the masculine's energy to shape them. They need to embody their own mature inner masculine and his strong boundaries. It's not about blaming men (immature feminine), it's about first creating inner trust with your own masculine. As you learn to trust your mature (emphasizing mature) masculine, then you will find it easier to trust, and surrender to another's. And by developing your˙ mature masculine, you will be creating the skills and awareness needed to help others hold and develop their masculine energy.

When we hold hate and vengeance for another, they have power over us. It is our hateful thoughts and inability to accept another for who they are, that stops our evolution and their transformation. Forgiveness opens the heart and allows us to take our power back.

By *surrendering to ourselves* to our own Karma, to the story of our life, the pain of our past, what we resist feeling and what we judge as good and bad, we heal ourselves and allow ourselves the power to transform. In certain moments, when we feel safe enough to *surrender to another* (not to ourselves), to someone we trust, we are able to generate energy with the other that is different to our own energy, circulating it between us, we make love to each other as opposed to fucking each other, independently of any sexual acts.

Surrender is Power and Trust is Forgiveness.

Trust Is Forgiveness

Trust and forgiveness share the same emotional frequency and they both hold some of the hardest lessons to learn. When we reflect on life, we will often see that it is the people who we trust that hurt us the most. If in trusting someone we believe it means that they will never do anything wrong, or hurt us again, directly or indirectly, then we are being naïve. To trust someone is to say yes to life, yes to experiencing both pleasure and pain through the experiences that they bring. One perspective on trust would say: *When we tell someone "I trust you", we are indirectly saying, "You are worthy of my forgiveness", although we may feel differently if and when they hurt us.*

This perspective can go against the phrase, *"No one can hurt you, you can only hurt yourself."* This phrase deals with non-physical aspects of life, and it helps us to take responsibility for ourselves. But when we love someone, we allow ourselves to be vulnerable to their actions. If we did not allow ourselves to be vulnerable, it would mean that we never really trusted them. So, when they act from their immature, we are likely to feel hurt; how we choose to deal and learn from this hurt is a demonstration of our own personal development. The phrase is true in the sense that we only ever hurt ourselves, as everything is a reflection of the self, but this view is not helpful when we are living in duality, in separation, here to experience joy through connection. Saying I feel hurt by your actions, while deeply knowing that we created it, serves us and the other more, as they have the feedback that they need to change.

Vulnerability Is a Path to Strength

To be vulnerable, we have to be brave enough to know that we can feel hurt and pain, break down, and then put ourselves back together.

If we are scared of being vulnerable or we are constantly avoiding it, we may not feel safe or strong enough to face ourselves in this way, to face our weaker parts. We can see that vulnerability, bravery, strength, victimhood, and cowardice all share a similar vibrational frequency. Putting these emotions onto the polarity framework, shows us that to move from bravery to strength, we need our vulnerability and to move from victimhood or cowardice to vulnerability, we need strength. Language here might work differently for different people and situations, but the premise remains the same, that if we are not brave enough to surrender to the negative wrongness and darkness of ourselves and in part, to the negative wrongness and darkness of others, then it means we are too afraid of our pain and too afraid of our reflection, so we cannot help to heal the world or evolve collective consciousness.

To help heal the world and evolve collective consciousness, we have to go back into our immature and start to make it healthy, along with all of our desires, so that when we do break down, we are able to trust our own integrity and authenticity to create beauty in the world and act with humanity. This is one way that shadow work can make us both vulnerable and strong.

Forgiveness in the Mind

The relationship between our physical, emotional, and mental bodies is not always straight forward. Asking the mind to forgive before we have an integrated relationship with our self, is like asking a mathematician to agree that $1 + 1 = 3$.

The mental body can struggle with the paradoxes from which we are made. When we are in our immature expressions, we are more likely to think linearly, making abstract concepts that hold greater truth impossible to understand. The body has an innate wisdom and understanding, it knows what to trust. On a vibrational spectrum, trust is akin to discernment and knowing, meaning that the body just "knows" and we need to learn to trust it.

Once we have self-trust, then the universe will reflect back to us a reality that we can trust. But our lessons in life still need to be learned, so after someone has broken our trust, in order to give it back to them, we need to find a way to forgive.

Worthy of Our Own Forgiveness

Learning to work with the dynamic of trust and forgiveness with others is important, but this dynamic also needs to be present within ourselves. Life looks differently when we have self-trust and feel worthy of our own forgiveness (or at the very least, know that this is possible). For some people, forgiving others leads us to forgiving ourselves, and for others, forgiving ourselves leads us to forgiving others.

Trust is primarily found in the body and through our breath. As we learn to breathe deeply into our stomach, we learn to trust our emotions more and the information in our physical body, and in turn the mind relaxes.

The truth is that it's not safe to be in a body. We can get hurt, we can lose our job, our money, become homeless, or there could be a war. But by believing it's not safe, we create more fear, we make it unsafe. We either attract the actual things that we are scared of or we create so much protection and prevention against these things that we can no longer live (another twist in the polarity framework that stops our physical, mental, and emotional alignment). The only way to break this contradiction is to lie to ourselves. To tell our bodies that life is safe. The truth is that we are free to live, love, and be happy when we believe that we are.

This is the same with our heart. When we trust people with our hearts, we open ourselves up to being vulnerable, so we can get hurt. But it's only by trusting people that they can become trustworthy. So trust, trust and trust some more, and when it hurts like hell, trust that the pain is what we need right now.

De-armouring Our Heart

Unlike our bodies, our hearts never really break, they can be ripped open, but then the choice is ours to close or grow back stronger. The only thing that stops us from loving less than before is the memory and fear of how much it hurt last time. This is the armour in our body. If we've burnt our hand on a candle or been hit by a truck, the body automatically flinches when these things come close. When we have armour around our heart and a potential new love comes close, we are likely to do the same on the subconscious level, and push them away because we remember the pain.

With an aligned physical, mental, and emotional body, we can choose to act differently. We can choose to treat our heart like a muscle, with heartbreak simply giving us a greater capacity for love, because to forgive, takes a big heart, and to forgive the unforgivable, simply means we need to make our heart bigger (achieving this or not achieving this is *not* as important as working towards it).

When the Masculine and Feminine Polarity Framework is used as part of an integrative therapy practice, there is a tool called *dialogue work,* that really helps with forgiveness. It helps to take us out of the story while not losing the emotional charge. We are not necessarily looking for answers or solutions in this process, as generally there are none other than to forgive. But in relation to forgiveness, through dialogue work, we enable two important things to happen:

1 We wake up the emotional trauma in the body, finding where it is stored on the cellular level, and this often relates to existing physical illnesses or misalignments.
2 We start to understand that when we need to forgive someone else, there is something within us in our masculine or feminine, generally related to our mother or father, that is unhealthy, damaged, and immature. We might be attached to this thing or rejecting it, but once we understand what it is, we enable forgiveness for our self and the other.

A whole book could be written on what the depth dialogue work brings from the non-dual perspective. Developed from Gestalt therapy, with relations to another therapy technique called Aspecting, the real learnings from this work come from experiencing and translating the story from the mind to the physical and emotional bodies, and then back to the mind again. The process allows us to understand and heal generations of trauma by embodying perspectives that are not our own but forgiving them as if they were.

27
The Healthy Victim
~

We all have the archetype of victim within us, even if it rarely comes out. So, the correct question to ask is, *"How do I make the victim (or at least this victim type of energy) inside of me healthy?"* To some this might sound like the craziest question in the world, but most of our immature aspects have a healthy and beneficial side: healthy competition is easier to see and arrogance will turn into deserved respect before moving into mature humbleness; the healthy victim is an expression of unconditional love and trust, while providing the energy from which life is created but without actually losing anything because the mind is not judging so harshly or locked in polarity.

On the internal level, it's quite easy to see what most of us do, we suffer "now" for pleasure "later", going to a job we hate in order to provide for our family and the people we love. We don't often see these kinds of actions as sacrifices, the ones we make for love, as *"being a victim"*, but to better understand this energy and what's really going on inside of us, on a deeper level, it is helpful.

For most of us, when a desire arises related to being a victim (often with a sexual connotation), we suppress it, we judge it as bad and in that moment, if such a thing as bad existed, it probably would be. But on the heart level, being a victim does not really exist, the heart just wants to give to life, to create love. It does not recognize or experience separation in the same way as the mind. The heart wants to trust implicitly, to trust in life and the more it gives to life, the more love there is in the world, thus the more love there is for the heart to experience.

Put simply, the heart believes that to receive love, you give love, and everything is love.

Energy flowing from one heart/chakra/energy centre to another, on an energetic level, is the feminine giving to the masculine, the masculine then gives back to the feminine in a different way, *but this is much more about polarity work on an energetic level than it is healing an unhealthy victim mentality.*

Current reality means that it is not safe for the heart to give like this, life would just become unbalanced, so the mind stops us from giving, to stop us from being a victim. And this immediately creates mis-alignment with the heart and mind, wanting different things so the mind closes the heart so as not to be a victim and we stay safe. If we're all able to trust and give love freely without fear of getting hurt or wondering how and where love will come back, then the world would be a very different place, but currently the balance between polarity and duality in our world is very different, and right now that's how it is meant to be, otherwise it would be different.

When the heart gives to life fully, it orgasms, the whole body orgasms. On the genital level, for both men and women, an orgasm brings our energy to earth, sexual fluids in sex magic are key to manifestation, so what the heart desires is manifested and created in reality (this works so much better when there is a connection with another, but it's not essential), so to *cum* from the heart for another, is to cum, or come, to earth for their desires.

But often the mind stops us from giving to life in this way, from orgasming from our heart, to fully give love to another. Sometimes the mind, or our unhealthy ego and inner critic, work against us in this way, making sure that when we cum, our sexual desires and fantasies are dark and connected to being a victim or abusing another, and making them the victim, so we start to lock ourselves into separation, which brings us into the unhealthy ego and cuts us off from our power.

If our lower three chakras or energy centres are unhealthy, then so are our desires. The alignment between our sex, heart, and mind is not there because we don't understand ourselves. In shadow work, most of our sexual fantasies have a different meaning to what we would immediately presume them to be, and they often work in reverse and in riddles, similar to how we dream so we each need to interpret our shadow and sexual fantasies differently.

Examples:
- To be raped, could be the desire to take our power back, but it could also be to surrender, or it could be to have the masculine take everything away that we feel ashamed of energetically: including memories, images, and feelings that we would not want to share with a lover, so we feel ashamed and unworthy, and thus never fully surrender these parts of ourselves, so we fantasize about being raped, subconsciously desiring someone to take these aspects of our self away.
- Degrading fetishes and fetishes about certain body parts are often about loving the lower parts of another person or ourselves, to say that

every part of you is worthy and beautiful (even if the fantasy is the total reverse, the polarity of what we need).

- The desire to kill or to be killed in sex is often the longing for the death of our ego, not our actual body.

As we heal the traumas in our lower energy centres, we start to understand ourselves more and our fantasies become aligned to what we really want; this does not mean that we cannot play with our shadow if we enjoy it, sexual stimulation is healthy and our dark side is here to help us evolve (but not consume us). Once we have done this work, truly done it, we will be left with similar problems, but able to see them in a different light. When we invest our time into relationships, our mind will want to see balance and safety, but sometimes momentary unbalance *(heartbreak)*, is what serves us the most in the long term.

There are no right answers here, but an evolved understanding of ourselves will help us to make better choices. Once we know that our heart opens through giving and we are integrated enough to live both our masculine and feminine polarities simultaneously, then heartbreak can become heart-opening and the act of giving in this way of orgasming from the heart and *cumming* to earth can offer us so much, especially when we are not dependent on another, but free.

Exploring topics of surrender, control, domination, submission, and victimhood from this place can help us heal our shadow and support us to surrender in the moments when we know we are truly loved and cared for: coming to earth should be a blissful experience. So, the healthy victim is not a victim at all, although from the outside looking in, it may be misjudged. The healthy victim is someone who understands the polarities of life and trusts in their higher self implicitly: they know that you need to give in order to get, and that loving and forgiving unconditionally enables the universe, source, or God to create beauty and provide the gifts of life in unexpected ways.

Part 3

SHADOW WORK

The Immature's Shadow

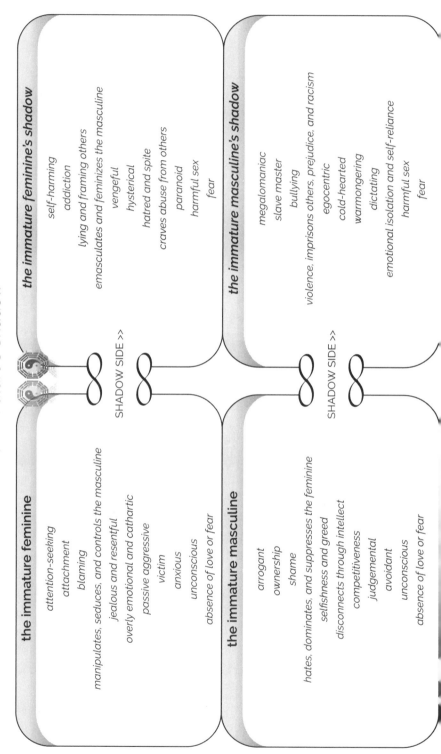

the immature feminine

- attention-seeking
- attachment
- blaming
- manipulates, seduces, and controls the masculine
- jealous and resentful
- overly emotional and cathartic
- passive aggressive
- victim
- anxious
- unconscious
- absence of love or fear

SHADOW SIDE >>

the immature feminine's shadow

- self-harming
- addiction
- lying and framing others
- emasculates and feminizes the masculine
- vengeful
- hysterical
- hatred and spite
- craves abuse from others
- paranoid
- harmful sex
- fear

the immature masculine

- arrogant
- ownership
- shame
- hates, dominates, and suppresses the feminine
- selfishness and greed
- disconnects through intellect
- competitiveness
- judgemental
- avoidant
- unconscious
- absence of love or fear

SHADOW SIDE >>

the immature masculine's shadow

- megalomaniac
- slave master
- bullying
- violence, imprisons others, prejudice, and racism
- egocentric
- cold-hearted
- warmongering
- dictating
- emotional isolation and self-reliance
- harmful sex
- fear

28
The Shadow

Our Shadow allows us to recognize light and gives us a direction to move; when we are unconsciously acting from our shadow, we are simply acting from fear. Recognizing our shadow is recognizing our fears, seeing the helpfulness of them, and how they serve us.

When evolution is stuck, our shadow gives an extra layer of depth that helps us work with polarity and duality, that helps us work specifically with:

- the mature and immature;
- the healthy and unhealthy;
- and of course, the masculine and feminine.

Our shadow can be viewed as a more extreme expression of our unhealthy immature, with little to no tangible healthy aspects. Very rarely does it serve us to take life to such dark extremes, but sometimes it does and at the very least, an understanding of what is going on can help us.

When our immature behaviour is very strong and the beliefs we hold about it are continuously being reinforced by our environment, then our immature can devolve further: in Masculine and Feminine Polarity Work, we call this "the shadow", and it is aligned closely with the work of Carl Jung (1875–1961) founder of analytical psychology, who originally used the term shadow in relation to the subconscious mind.

There are few straight answers when working to evolve our shadow. The human psyche is complex and we might need to be creative with our use of Masculine and Feminine Polarity Work and other tools that help deal with deep-rooted problems and addictions. Many tools and techniques exist in the world of shadow work and we will explore some of these in the following chapters. The book, Feeding Your Demons: Ancient Wisdom for Resolving Inner Conflict, by Tsultrim Allione, is a good option for transforming our shadows, whereas Masculine and Feminine Polarity Work focuses on the overall theme and role of our shadow in relation to polarity and duality.

29
Four Schools of Shadow Work

Through my work and practice I identified two main schools of shadow work, the second school I break up into three categories, so it's easier to say 2nd-, 3rd-, and 4th-level shadow work although all of these levels are of the 2nd school.

1st level: Integrate your shadow.
2nd level: Maintain a healthy amount of shadow to generate power.
3rd level: Develop purity of heart.
4th level: Working in the collective consciousness.

The first school is to love, integrate and heal our shadows, turning darkness into light. This is the more mainstream approach and for many people shadow work stops here.

The second approach, school or level of shadow work often creates negative reactions as it is teaching us to maintain a healthy amount of shadow which we draw power from.

3rd-level shadow work is about developing purity of heart, and should never be taken lightly and 4th-level shadow work is in the realms of the collective consciousness.

In all shadow work, we are working to make the unconscious conscious, reducing the veil between our subconscious and conscious mind and also our higher self. As we reduce the barrier between the subconscious and conscious mind communication with ourself changes: we understand ourselves better, the reality and the matrix that we live, the nature of time, and we are likely to become more psychic. Meditation helps with this too but shadow work takes the fear of who we truly are away, while transforming the parts of ourselves that we may be afraid of.

Listening to our intuition means allowing more encompassing and higher parts of ourselves to teach and guide us. Shadow work supports this process by teaching us not to be afraid of our lower self but to make it healthy and integrate it.

2nd- and 3rd-level shadow work are related and interchangeable and 4th-level shadow work happens in the collective consciousness. You don't need to work up through the levels as in 1, 2, 3 and 4, you just need to trust yourself to apply what is best at any given time.

4th-level shadow work is teaching us compassion, to understand others, the pain that drove them to bad choices and some of the soul and life lessons that lay beyond their pain. 4th-level shadow work teaches us oneness and non-separation beyond a mental concept and starts to give us an embodied understanding and true knowledge, unexplainable knowledge as to what oneness is. Working in the collective consciousness is also a great way to learn more about and develop ourselves, reducing our ego and coming to understand more of how reality is created.

Shadow work in general teaches us to appreciate paradoxical situations and find wisdom within them and to live our life from a multi-dimensional perspective, with a non-dual mind that is committed to both evolution and balance. By always focusing on evolution and balance together in shadow work we remain safe—with the polarity framework being a useful mental guide or map for managing evolution in a balanced way. The polarity framework teaches us to use polarity with duality in order to suffer less and to ensure that when we do suffer we evolve, eventually changing our relationship with suffering entirely though developing a non-dual mind.

To deny suffering completely, or to be afraid of suffering is foolish. Our rejection of suffering will make us suffer, our attachment to suffering will make us suffer and even our non-attachment to suffering can work out badly as until we are living in an enlightened Buddha-like state, non-attachment to suffering is very often our rejection of suffering.

To be happy we actually need all three: rejection, attachment and non-attachment to our suffering (remembering that body de-armouring teaches our body non-attachment to suffering). None of them are right and none of them are wrong, it's just about looking at how and when we apply each: attachment, rejection and non-attachment, and still being fluid, with no hard and fast rules.

One of the hardest parts of finding alignment is looking at our shadows. To keep alignment between our heart, mind and sex, we cannot have any resistance to our desires, on any level.

But the truth is that we often have resistance, and if we always resist a certain part of ourselves, what we judge as bad and deem to be incorrect, then our energy becomes stuck and stagnant. So when we are in a stuck place, often doing the wrong thing, becomes the right thing.

The Shadow Work chapters in this book, in my mind, build on from Jungian phycology (you could call Carl Jung the Godfather of shadow work psychology, who I would say was more of a mainstream mystic thus some people prefer Sigmund Freud's work over Jung's) and both are a good introduction to some of the more controversial approaches in the world of shadow work, while still covering the basics.

30
Emphasizing Our Shadow

Emphasizing our shadow comes with risks. Most of us already have enough shadow to transform, so we do not need to create more. But an understanding of our shadow, and that of others, greatly benefits us in using the laws of polarity and duality. When something can kill us or put us in great danger, we develop some form of respect for it because we value our life. We also gain knowledge and understanding about its risks as well as its benefits. Shadow work is much the same, the more we dare to understand our shadow, the more knowledge and benefits we gain. So, when we choose to go into darker places, with awareness, it serves our growth. But often the natural human desire to explore our shadow sends us into these places without awareness and consciousness. As a consequence, we risk losing a part of ourselves, being seduced by darker influences, reducing our free will and forgetting why we chose to explore certain sides of our self with the company and people we now find ourselves with.

Shadow work without authenticity and integrity is dangerous and it can diminish our free will.

We might consciously or subconsciously choose to emphasize our shadow when we feel that there is not enough conflict, emotion, passion, or fire in our life to break through into higher vibrational and more fulfilling experiences. Life is okay, our job is okay, family is okay, we are okay, but the general feeling of life is being stuck. By using our darker side, or our shadow, we can go into our anger and other emotions, amplifying and increasing these so that we can feel more passion and use it to create breakthroughs in other areas of our life.

Shadow work is often connected to our sexuality, with sex being the ultimate expression of polarity, with the power to create life. Repressed sexual desires, the ones we judge as bad, viewed in a different light are often messages from our subconscious or higher self. There is something for us to learn, normally related to our relationship to polarity *(how we work with duality on the Masculine and Feminine Polarity Framework)*, and psychology *(our personal conditioning—normally from childhood, our beliefs, and our behaviours)*. But the more we repress our primal and animal instincts, the more twisted or even perverted they can become.

But not all shadow work is sexual, as the maps show, every immature trait has a shadow aspect: *our extremely unhealthy and immature.* If we venture deeply into our shadows, we might find ourselves in sub-cultures of society, from sex clubs, to fight clubs, to non-peaceful forms of activism, and protest, to underground music scenes, American redneck festivals, death metal, mosh dance pits, and goth, magik, or Wicca communities. Some of these places attract people consciously working on their shadow, as well as very grounded people who subconsciously know that they need this kind of release to create balance. Many people just crave to experience negativity, loss, pain suffering and darkness as a way to create balance, as a way of the most basic form of emotional alchemy.

Unfortunately, there are also those who are there simply because they are lost, confused, and consumed by their shadow and self-destructive behaviours due to the traumas in their life and negative energies and entities that control them, through fear to do bad or violent things to themselves or others, and in my simple world view, these people need support to work on themselves with tools like the ones in this book while living in a healthy and supportive environment.

Actively working on our shadow desires is not necessarily a *"bad"* or *"evil"* thing. *But the reality is, "bad" and "evil" things happen when our vibration and desires match them,* so we need to be very careful and for most of us, there is a better way. For people who are lost in their shadow, the laws of attraction and vibration can have a detrimental effect, with the vibration of these people becoming heavier and more negative. Duality will always counteract this polarization, offering hope and a way out, a way back to a higher vibration, but a lot of willpower is required to take it. Hopefully, understanding why some people become trapped in their shadow gives us another reason not to judge: be it they need to learn something by being there, or that they simply lack the knowledge and understanding to make positive change.

We don't know why someone is choosing something and a certain path in life. All we can do is try to understand and trust that their path is right for them and act in a way that helps their evolution. We should not impose what we think is best, as this is normally an unhealthy form of domination and manipulation from our immature. And of course, there are moments where our domination of a situation or our manipulation/co-creation of it, can be the healthiest and most needed thing, *but this can be very hard to tell without good intuition and knowing: our common sense is often flawed when our soul is looking for deeper meaning.*

When entering into shadow work, it is important that we are not susceptible to guilt and shame, but that we have a strong masculine. A weak masculine has a weak will that can bend and we are most likely to lose ourselves. We can discover a lot about ourselves by finding *activities in subcultures with much higher vibrations committed to self-development and personal transcendence,* helping us transcend the predominance of the immature masculine that is still found in most traditional and recreational activities: a lot of these groups, more *committed to self-development and personal transcendence,* actively do shadow work in a more conscious and transformative way:

Plant medicine, shamanic practices, tantric and conscious sexuality festivals, some yogic communities, polyamours and other intentional communities, circling groups, process-orientated psychology, and other self-development groups to name but a few, generally all have a large focus on shadow work but do not emphasize it in extreme or intense ways.

As we reframe our shadow and darkness in a potentially positive way, our relationship to judgement changes and we can take a more encompassing perspective. As we become more conscious, our unconscious fears transform and as we gain more awareness, our shadow is no longer a nasty place: the shade can be a nice place on a hot and sunny day.

A simpler, less risky way to do shadow work, is through fantasy and role-play. Finding all the archetypes inside of us that we judge as negative, then acting them out and giving them space can help us understand ourselves more. Using imagination and fantasy in this way can be a powerful tool for self-understanding and transformation. Acting classes, improvised theatre jams, and other creative groups that allow us to express these shadow parts of ourselves in a light and fun way can also be wonderful.

However many people need a level of human sexuality in their shadow expressions to fully benefit. When we don't have this, we risk not fully expressing ourselves, thus not achieving our full potential. Finding our fully aligned and authentic self is hard, if not impossible when expressions of our sexuality are missing. If expressions are missing because we have guilt and shame towards our sexual desires, then to find our aligned and authentic self, we need a safe space to transform these shadow-related sexual desires, taking the feelings of guilt and shame away, leaving us with healthy sexual desires.

When we are fearless and conscious at the same time, we realize our dark side is a gift, and using it correctly is an art.

Within some intentional communities and eco-villages, a tool called "Forum" is used. It allows creative expressions in all areas of life and relationships to be played out in public, including sexual affairs. Through role-play and drama, the group experiences different sides and perspectives of a situation causing conflict or pain, so everyone in the group has a more expanded awareness. Anger towards a person or situation is displayed in a more fun way. Jealousy is acted out in situations to create resonance, so people can take their own learnings from their fellow community members.

This allows us to see that the story or drama in our life is not really us, it is a shared theme that we all can learn and benefit from. It gives multiple perspectives to a situation quickly, allowing deeper personal answers to emerge. Emotions are generally high, with a prevailing sense of fun, and each participant experiencing a wide and mixed spectrum of emotion.

The conscious sexuality movement and festivals are also making a lot of headway in pioneering ways for humans to be together, while accepting and looking at their shadow. Although these groups seem to have a lot of their own shadow, they are mostly transparent about their failures and learnings in the work of conscious human sexuality. It's important to have a strong masculine in these groups, otherwise becoming a victim is a real risk. But at the same time, a lot of what these groups teach is about developing the masculine and feminine principles.

Understanding the more extreme ways to do shadow work can allow our minds to understand the importance of it, which then helps us to not feel silly during such acting, role-playing, and forum circles. Some of us will never need to emphasize our shadow; knowing about it and then transforming what we have, is generally enough.

It's irresponsible to go too deeply into 3rd- and 4th-level shadow work until the concepts within the polarity framework have been mastered, and until one has actual experience of integrating shadows. Shadow work itself is paradoxical and needs to be learned experientially if one is to transform and evolve in a healthy and balanced way. Mastering the basics of shadow work is important and needs to happen before deciding if we individually need to integrate deeper shadow work into our lives: not everyone does. It's helpful to keep in mind that 3rd-level shadow work is about developing purity of heart and that 4th-level shadow work is about working with the collective consciousness. By holding these higher ideals and aspirations in more basic shadow work we allow more integrity when integrating and giving meaning to our existing shadows.

31
Transforming Our Shadow

It helps to have influences of both the mature masculine and feminine when evolving shadows, but sometimes focusing on an immature expression is helpful too. When dealing with the masculine's immature shadow, the mature feminine will provide the qualities that the masculine needs to move back to his mature expression. The mature masculine will act as the role model for the immature masculine and his shadow, or the father or mentor to the tyrant boy. Looking at this example the other way around, the mature feminine would be the mother to the spoiled girl.

When we are secure in our mature expression (unlike in previous examples where the immature moves the opposing mature down), the immature masculine may not be able to bring the mature feminine down and the immature feminine may not be able to bring the mature masculine down either. Instead, the immature simply moves into his or her shadow, leaving the opposing polarity in their mature (it's good to read this again to ensure it's understood: *instead, the immature simply moves into his or her shadow, leaving the opposing polarity in their mature*).

The positive qualities, attributes, mindsets, and beliefs of the mature, have become so hardwired into the person's psyche, that it's fundamental to who they are. Their behaviour is likely to be reactive *as opposed* to mindful, but still demonstrating mature traits. Reactive behaviour in the mature is often an expression of an unhealthy mature. This is one potential repercussion of using hypnosis and other methods of reprogramming the subconscious mind, before we have actually learned the lessons that our shadow and immature self are teaching us. Methods such as hypnosis can be helpful, we just have to be careful not to misuse them and not to reprogramme our subconscious mind with states of being that we are not holistically ready for.

If we took away all of our shadow and immature aspects, we would have taken away our pain, pain that is there to teach us and help us evolve. The desired behaviour may now be there and this certainly can bring one level of success, but our personality is likely to be shallow and our ego missing depth, substance, and most importantly, genuine compassion.

This is much more akin to using our brain as a computer, rather than expanding consciousness to be more than the mind and more than the ego.

When using hypnosis and other methods to work with our subconscious, it's wise to make sure we are taking all the gifts that life is offering us and actually learning from our experiences. Life is a lesson, and our pain is a great teacher, which means it's much better to embrace our pain than to run from it.

"The cure for the pain is the pain." – Jalal ad-Din Muhammad Rumi, 1207 to 1273.

Example

Take "The Mirror" diagram out if you find anything hard to follow.

Looking at a man with a very mature masculine, who is generally wise and has good emotional and mental balance, but suddenly experiences heartbreak:

His immature feminine will try to take him into victimhood, *normally as an unhealthy expression.*

If his mature masculine does not have the wisdom and insight, to evolve his immature feminine from her victim expression back to her creative and auspicious mature expression, he is able to stay in his mature masculine out of familiarity.

Staying in the mature out of familiarity instead of mindfulness, creates shadow. As the rest of his mature masculine is available with integrity and discernment, his feminine returns to mainly being in her mature also. His mature feminine loves and accepts all that is, so she loves and accepts the feminine's new immature shadow too.

The immature feminine's victim shadow craves abuse through various means. This could be drinking, gambling, pornography, over-eating, and all other known and unknown forms of self-abuse, masculine or feminine related. Consciously or unconsciously, the man starts looking from his feminine shadow for other people to hurt him, to recreate the experience of pain, because unconsciously he knows that he needs the pain to heal. As the Rumi quote tells us, *"The cure for the pain is the pain."*

He goes further and further into his pain as this is what his subconscious mind believes will evolve the depths of his mature masculine. He goes into his feminine shadow so that his mature masculine can realize what he's done, wake up, and evolve, or for him to move into his mature feminine and then heal his feminine shadow in a similar way *(you will know which way is right for you at the time)*. This is a common subconscious mental pattern, playing out that can help us learn from our pain, unfortunately in this case, his mature masculine is too paralyzed to help and his mind has created rules and beliefs that prevent him from seeing a healthy solution or way out.

Two other things are also going on that do not help this process:

1 The first are the laws of vibration and attraction. Simplified, this means that what we vibrate on, we will attract. So, if we vibrate on abuse, think about abuse, keep reliving and thinking about our traumatic memories of abuse, we will attract more abuse. Whereas if we have always had love, money, joy, and happiness, we will continue to attract, love, money, joy, and happiness.

2 The second is the conservation law of energy, or the first law of thermodynamics. It states that in a closed system, energy cannot be created or destroyed, it can only transform.

Energy will follow patterns and repeat itself until transformation happens. Neurological patterns in our brains repeat over and over again and this can make our unhealthy and reactive ego feel safe, as it has a reference for what is happening. Unfortunately, our ego's subconscious feels safe through familiarity and this creates addictions and unhealthy reactional behaviours. It does not matter how much a person "wants" to change, if they do not "know how" to change, and on a deeper level learn the lessons that their trauma and pain is there to teach them.

Often people will deal with just the vibration, or just the mental programming, but it's important to also find the lesson in the pain, that which makes us a bigger, wiser, better, stronger, version of ourselves. When our foundations are built on the knowledge of our own life experience, our mature masculine is able to stand for and encompass all that we are. We can hold our boundaries because we know ourselves and what is true for us. Actions that come from inner knowing are so much more powerful than authoritative actions which come from intellect.

In the above example, the man's masculine stays mostly in the Mature expression. The ideals of his mature feminine are still expressed to the outside world, so he may appear to be doing great with no shadow aspects at all. From here, his shadow is likely to start to manifest further self-destructive behaviours and addictions; this is one of the reasons why statements such as, "the more light you become, the more dark you become", sound true for so many people, because to an extent it is true, especially when we have an unhealthy mature that is creating more shadow, so that it can evolve. But it is definitely not "the truth" and there are far more healthy perspectives and truths to adopt that help us live our lives.

In our close love relationships and with our parental figures, it is easier to see that what we reject about them is normally somewhere within us. *If we have developed enough conscious awareness, we will also see that what we reject about ourselves is often in their shadow.* The more we notice that rejecting another is rejecting ourselves, we start to take our power back, the power that we have been blocking ourselves from, so we no longer need to be trapped in a victim mentality with the black and white picture of duality that this creates.

We become the master and the architect of our life.

We may notice the partial truths that we have held in the past become stronger, like they are fighting to be validated, fighting for attention and time. The truth that says, "for every positive thought we have, that we have to create a negative thought", may try and shift our consciousness back, back into a more black and white reality. Always remember that both are true some of the time, *but* not all of the time, and what is true most of the time, solely depends on our choices and free will, and it's totally okay for the whole of the human race to believe that life is 80 to 90% more, love, joy, and happiness than it is pain.

Life is multi-dimensional and the only thing that is "wrong" is believing that we know the truth, or that our God is supreme, because this stops us experiencing life, experiencing God, and growing as a person. We should use these internal battles and feelings as a test, a test to our commitment to the positive visions and aspirations that we have imagined. We always have choice and we always have free will, being able to use our choice and free will is a case of getting out of our unhealthy ego and into our healthy one, regardless of whether we are choosing to be mature or immature in that moment.

Even wise, respected people, teachers, priests, gurus, and the like, who seem to have evolved and are acting from their mature and integrated self, can still have very big, self-destructive shadows as in the example above. Our shadow is just another expression of polarity and duality that needs to be learned from and healed to give rise to greater expressions of the individual, whether they are enlightened or not. Enlightened people still have egos, they still have a personality that expresses the uniqueness of their past. The immature shadow of the masculine is not expected to directly trigger the opposing immature shadow of the feminine. The immature and mature expressions commonly do this for each other in healthy and unhealthy ways, but the shadow is more complex and too misaligned from natural polarities to easily be understood by them. Although the polarity framework is a great tool for healing and transforming shadows, we have to be willing to work a little harder to apply it.

Archetypes

Archetypes are described by Carl Jung as *"highly developed elements of the collective unconscious"*. Jung defines twelve archetypes to work with, although in general terms and throughout human history and culture, the number of archetypes is limitless and the meaning of each somewhat personal to the individual. Many are predominately associated with the masculine or feminine, such as the maiden and the knight or the king and the queen.

Jung, also talked about the Anima and the Animus, as archetypes with the Anima being the part of the psyche which is directed inwards, in touch with the subconscious and the feminine part of a man's personality and the Animus, being the motivation to do something and the masculine part of a woman's personality.

At a certain point, archetypes become so complex that they cannot be predominately associated with the masculine or feminine anymore. For example:

- The Child, Orphan, Wounded Child, Inner Child
- The Lover
- The Clown, Jester, Tramp, Joker
- The Visionary, Creator, Revolutionary
- The Guide, Healer, Teacher
- The Seeker, Wanderer, Disciple, Dreamer

These archetypes are so complex that they will all show a mixture of the masculine and the feminine, the mature and the immature. It's very useful to think of archetypes that resonate with our situation when looking for solutions to evolve from our immature or our darker shadow self. However, we must remember that the meaning of an archetype and how our subconscious mind translates it, will always be individual to us and shaped by the knowledge and understanding that we have (at least until someone else tells us something different).

Although knight, king, queen, princess, witch, magician, and warrior are archetypes or roles often used in Western self-development, mysticism and psychology, each is stereotypically assigned to a gender, but by working to evolve these archetypes within ourselves or to understand how their dynamics play out in others, regardless of gender, reveals another level of the paradox that the polarity framework is trying to help us understand.

The best analogy for this is to see how all the archetypes in a deck of Tarot cards are designed to relate to and explain your life experiences, just as the 64 different life paths used in the iChing are (which is the cover of this book). By not limiting our minds with gender in archetype work and instead focusing on the integration of the archetype as a reflection of our own integration and understanding at the time, we give ourselves the gift of diversity and the best chance of growth.

In Buddhist Tibetan Tantra, monks meditate on pictures of deities, *divine expressions, and aspects of God,* until they feel that they can absorb the essence of these deities into themselves, becoming a divine expression of God. Hinduism works in a similar way, with the many Hindu Gods and Goddesses being seen as archetypes. Egypt is again similar, with multiple Gods representing different aspects of society; native Americans, Aborigines, and some parts of Africa, have more shamanic archetypes, drawing their way of experiencing life through animals and the natural world. In the West, we often draw our archetypes from more medieval times, expressing hierarchy and order through kings, queens, princesses, knights, priestesses, witches, wizards, warriors, lovers, and the like.

When working with archetypes, don't limit yourself to one culture or one way of being, the more we can include in our imagination to develop our subconscious mind, the more we can become conscious of and understand it. It's important that we always come back to a grounded sense of consensual reality after archetype work, otherwise we move too far away from the collective consciousness and consensus reality.

32

The Illusion of Good and Bad

Good and bad do not exist in duality, they are not a real polarity like day and night, masculine and feminine, or hot and cold. Good and bad are beliefs created from personal preferences and judgements that are normally relevant to a specific moment in time. Notice how we are not saying that, the "unhealthy immature" is bad: sometimes the immature is unhealthy and sometimes it is not. Being competitive, owning something, avoiding someone or something, or having a judgement, is not always "bad". Or when acting from the feminine, it's not always "bad" to have an attachment, to seduce, or at times to be anxious or have the desire for attention. We have to be authentic. From authenticity, transformation can arise:

Maybe we have a very good reason to feel anxious, and without that anxious feeling we may walk into a dangerous situation.

When we can let go of the mind and the unhealthy ego, allowing our authentic expression and the wisdom of our bodies to guide us, we can drop our beliefs of lack and unhappiness, our pain, our shame, and our conditioning:

Our desire for intimacy and the act of seducing a lover, might not come from our mature self, but can lead to some of the most precious moments of our life.

When we feel "bad" for being in our immature, we are creating a judgement that reinforces the immature behaviour. Feeling bad, guilty, and shameful, stops us learning our lessons and transforming. From a spiritual perspective, we may deem, *from an immature perspective, we may judge* many things as unhealthy, but from the perspective of living in duality, being human, and navigating conflict, sometimes we want or need to be competitive, as it makes us stronger. Losing can teach us so much; it can teach us the power within our humility and that it is arrogant to think that our way is always the best: through losing, although this is not the only way, the immature masculine eventually learns to release and accepts the mature masculine's cooperation and interdependence and the world desperately needs these two things.

The world needs cooperation and interdependence.

As we evolve the wars in the world: the wars for fairness, for justice, and democracy, and the wars for resources, power, and control, turn within.

We will create more tension, more polarity, more unrest, and more shadow, until eventually we find the mature masculine's win-win solutions, and we find inner peace, selflessness, self-acceptance, and self-love. Once we have these things within ourselves, they are reflected back to us by the world, and we may still hit conflict and create mini wars to help us evolve and develop, but for the most part, and from this point on, our life is to be enjoyed, so please never give up on yourself, no matter how hard it gets.

For this sense of love and peace to be reflected in the whole world in a tangible way, we need to meet a critical mass in the collective consciousness, so the more men and women there are who act and make choices from their mature masculine, informed by their feminine, the quicker we reach this critical mass and the quicker positive change will unfold within ourselves, within our families and partnerships, and on a global scale.

Ultimately, these three things are the same, and whenever we want to change ourselves, the ones we love, or the world, it is best to look for and take actions that serve both personal and planetary transformation.

Sometimes, we have attachments and these attachments can keep us stuck, trapped, and cut off from a deeper understanding of life, from bliss, pleasure, and joy. But other times, these attachments can give us the safety and security we need to be able to let go of what's stopping our growth, which means letting go of our attachments. This becomes much easier when we develop self-trust; trust in universal laws; trust in the reflective nature of the universe; and trust in that we are creating our reality from our inner vibration.

No mother should feel bad for feeling attached to their child's happiness. Ultimately, the less attachment a mother can have, the more freedom and happiness the child will attain. *But the only thing that we could view as wrong in this dynamic, is feeling bad for the attachment as this will surely make the attachment unhealthier than it was before.* The immature self is not good or bad, but it is often unhealthy, sometimes competitiveness is what we want and need and other times it is not. When competitiveness is unhealthy, we need to turn it into its healthy expression by having more access to all of our mature qualities and also looking at the opposite immatures in the feminine and how they are supporting our unhealthy behaviour.

Or, we need to evolve it. We evolve it, not by going into the mature expression of competitiveness in the masculine, which is selflessness, but by being in the opposite expression of competitiveness in the mature feminine, which is acceptance. Acceptance will turn unhealthy competitiveness into selflessness, an expression of the mature masculine. From here, it is also easier to come back to competitiveness and to look at how we make it healthy, as our competitive nature is no longer run by fear.

When we can compete from a place of fearlessness with relaxation and without stress, understanding that we are only ever in competition with ourselves and knowing, if we *do* need to "beat" another through our actions, then in doing so overall, we make them stronger, then we will have mastered, or are at least close to mastering, *healthy competition.*

The basic premise of how to evolve the immature to the mature and in doing so, making the immature healthy, is reiterated throughout this book, through various examples; it's why we say, *"the more feminine you want to be, the more masculine you need to be, and the more masculine you want to be, the more feminine you need to be."* The sooner we are able to experience acceptance from the feminine, making our immature healthy, then the sooner our integrated and higher self becomes more present in our daily life and we start to know who we really are, and that good and bad are merely illusions that we use to understand ourselves.

Cycling through Pleasure and Pain

Each time we move through cycles of highs and lows, we gain greater awareness. These cycles could be a mix of masculine and feminine, pleasure and pain, attachment or detachment, and any other polarity that fits with our life. The pain we experience in life is shaped by our understanding, our attachments, and our judgements. By approaching life from a place of acceptance, we create authentic and sustained happiness, happiness that is not reliant on us or someone else being miserable. Happiness that is not destroyed when seemingly "bad" things happen. Authentic happiness is akin to raising our vibration with the ability to create depth and diversity. When we avoid pain and are attached to happiness, we become stuck, we cannot raise our vibration, so we bounce between a limited range of emotions.

Our rejection of pain and our attachment to pleasure is what keeps us trapped in our immature and shadow traits.

The mature feminine is naturally happy, as she accepts and embraces all of life with no judgement, which is key to our transformation. Pleasure and joy can be found in our tears and our rage when we have less judgements and more acceptance, especially when our inner masculine is mature, thus mindful, and can observe, allowing our feminine more space to express.

33
The Shadow in Society and Feminism

The realization and understanding that how we treat other people directly reflects how we treat ourselves, is becoming much more common and accepted. The Bible, the Koran, the Vedas, and other religious texts have been telling us this for thousands of years. From this perspective, when we see people acting from their immature, the correct thing to do is to act from our mature to help them evolve.

Unfortunately, there is a fine line between this and manipulation. However, if a person feels attacked or manipulated by us, it probably means that somewhere our immature or shadow is at play, or they have some serious narcissistic tendencies and a big shadow. Waiting until we are perfect before helping others is not practical, but we should know ourselves well enough so that when we do act, we actually help. Obviously if we see acts of abuse, we may want to and should act, regardless of how ready we feel. Expressing our immature in a very unhealthy way might be the correct course of action if it's the best we can manage at the time.

Actions from the immature have given rise to many needed movements in society that have been dealing with the larger collective shadow from feminism to the end of the apartheid, workers' strikes, to equal rights, and civil war. The driving forces and ideals in these movements often come from mature expressions, but it's the immature on the battlefield. No matter the race, gender, pay bracket, country, or religion that just won a war, in every scenario it is the immature masculine dominating the outcome.

The only way we can truly create change on a global scale, is to evolve ourselves and the collective consciousness. Societal systems need to become an expression and reflection of the mature masculine and feminine.

Looking at the maps, we can see that for a long period of human history the shadow of the masculine has had most of the power and influence over humanity. Fortunately, this is starting to change and we can see many more mature expressions of the masculine and feminine in our world. It's really important not to bastardize the masculine and over-emphasize the feminine. The mature feminine in all of us is crucial to supporting sustained global change, but the mature feminine can only fully rise with the mature masculine. Without one, we cannot have the other. The mature masculine has been rare in our world, especially in positions of power. But this is finally changing.

A time where we can all celebrate masculine energy, instead of being fearful of it, has begun.

Feeling guilt for being a man or being masculine, or having hate towards men and masculine traits will only slow this process down. As does being a woman and trying to balance power by acting from the masculine. It's not the gender that is important in this dynamic.

Feminism

If a woman feels her feminine is marginalized and she fights it in the old style of feminism by being more masculine, this actually reduces her femininity and supports the dominance of the immature masculine. The "fight" actually has nothing to do with being a man or a woman, it just feels that way because of how the predominant traits manifest through gender. Men are naturally conditioned to be more masculine and women naturally conditioned to be more feminine, so in an immature society, men have more power. We must realize this was never a war about gender, but the nature and dynamic of the immature masculine is to create separation and suppress others to have *power-over* others. This dynamic is in all of us and until we accept it within ourselves, we cannot make it healthy, we cannot transform it or make it healthy in the greater whole. It's the mature feminine that needs to act the most in this scenario, and in doing so she will create the rise of the mature masculine.

This is not to say that what has happened in our recent history about gender and equal rights has been wrong, it has been the process of change that needed to occur. In certain parts of the world this old style of feminism is still drastically needed as a pattern of change, there are probably better ways to act, but *when so much repression of the feminine is happening, it means that the immature masculine in both men and women are likely to fight. And in the short term, it's the immature masculine in women that needs to win for the good of all.*

Once this fight has been won and there is more or less equality between the sexes, as there is in a lot of the West, then we should no longer be looking to find equality in the sexes, but in masculine and feminine dynamics. Realizing that, the mature masculine is the most marginalized in society as he serves the economy the least, with money (the economy) largely controlling society. So it's in giving the mature masculine more time and space that women will benefit the most personally and in society: in a society where morals, values, human development and happiness comes closer to equalling economic and survival concerns. This process is a lot more complete in the West, complete enough in my mind at least, for women and the feminist movement to focus more on evolving men into their mature, opposed to fighting them from their immature. A world with more mature masculinity in both men and women would be a fairer and more balanced world.

34
The Backlash of Duality

Sometimes we can do everything right and nonetheless it feels like our demons are just getting bigger. This is a test from life, a test from ourselves to ourselves, to see if we are really ready for the shifts that we are creating.

As energy likes to repeat itself and to follow the same flow, so the mind likes to keep things familiar. Our subconscious and our unhealthy ego may try all kinds of mind games to keep us in old patterns of thinking, old vibrations that keep our flow of energy the same. Familiarity is the mental root of addiction, and the more mindful we are, the more we can witness our mind being addicted, and then choose to detach from it.

As we understand Masculine and Feminine Polarity Work and apply it to more of our life situations with integrated therapy techniques such as de-armouring, breathwork and energetic bodywork, we transform our old patterns, habits and behaviours with much more ease. The good thing to know is that if we are doing this work correctly and our shadow and demons feel like they are getting bigger, then it's working. As our vibration raises, we become aware of what was already in our shadow and we become more sensitive to it, so it affects us more. *Just beware not to create new shadows or reinforce old ones by overly focusing on what we judge as negative, instead of our healthy desires.*

As we choose to consciously work with creative tension and judge less, life gets easier. Tension in life brings new potentials, creative impulses and inspirations that guide our actions in the world. Sometimes we might feel locked into a balance of duality with each nice, good and healthy thing that we do compelling us to act negatively and unconsciously. The more yoga and meditation we do, the more we might desire to watch porn, eat cake, and drink alcohol because the unhealthy ego is fighting for the old vibration, the old familiar pattern. These can often feel like a fight to the death, but it is not actually us or our soul that dies, just the behavioural pattern created by our trauma. We need to find our own way of working with this, to apply self-discipline when it's needed and to give enough space to our unhealthy and shadow desires so that we are not suppressing them but seeing what they have to teach us. More often than not, responding to a backlash of duality is like most examples of using the Masculine and Feminine Polarity Framework, in that we need to:

- embody the opposing mature;
- evolve into the mature of that same polarity;
- avoid the opposing immature

as this develops our mature traits while making our immature healthy. In learning our lessons in life, very rarely is it one step forward and one step back, or worse, one step forward and two steps back. But sometimes it is. If this is the case, it's possible that we are being consumed by our shadow. Just as energy likes to follow the same pathways, occasionally when a negative thought pattern, energy, or entity gets stuck in our mind, it can be very hard for us to change. A mixture of integrative therapies and strategies are best here, such as de-armouring, breath, and energetic bodywork, remembering that for most of us, change is a gradual process, *with two steps forward and one step back often being the best way, as this means we have time to really integrate change.*

We should never be too disheartened if we move back into our immature or our shadow, as this is where tremendous growth happens. It simply means that we have more to learn and experience in life, it's an opportunity to grow, becoming and being more than we currently are. If we're ever really struggling, we should always seek help and look at the process as a *"dark night of the soul"*, a place where real radical transformation in our life can occur. Some people have more of these in their life than others. To quickly move into our aligned and integrated self, being left with no desire and no shadow is not why we are here. Buddha and a few others did it, but for most of us, it is not our path, not yet.

We are here to enjoy duality, to create life, beauty, and abundance from our pains and our passions and to watch the universe unfold as the creators of our own reality.

35
Dark Masculine and Feminine

The polarity framework is a model, a mental concept that helps us understand both duality and non-duality. It's not wrong and it's not right, there are other models out there that express polarity and/or just duality in different ways. The beauty of the polarity framework is its simplicity and how it expresses the paradox through its layers of masculine, feminine, mature, immature, healthy, unhealthy and shadow.

Some would say the masculine is always stable like the Sun so it's 1, always a full sun, never a half. And that the moon is sometimes full and sometimes new, so ever changing thus 2. The point of this example is to show us that different models give alternative views of duality, of deciphering reality, which our mind then uses to shape our experience of reality, of the fight between good and evil (if such a thing as evil were to exist), or put better, the dance. It is just that some models give us a wider perspective and others a narrower one.

In many cultures dark energy has been twisted and misunderstood, mainly through fear, but regardless of the reason, it stops us realizing the entirety of our being, of our light, and dark, how they work together, and thus give us power.

Through purely negative expressions of dark energy, many have denied what is beneficial in dark energy, leaving only violence, abuse, suffering, and other acts that we should reject instead of celebrate. All of life deserves to be celebrated, thus we need true and authentic manifestations of dark energy that are not evil, bad, or twisted by our own fear. These false expressions should not be celebrated because dark is not evil, just as light is not evil, nor is day and night, *evil is simply the construct of a mind trying to heal.*

Dark masculine and feminine energy have become distorted by the New Age movement, claiming many elements of what is dark and positive as all being of the light, thus darkness is viewed by many as mainly negative, and has been depleted of what is valuable, and thus we are creating an unbalanced and distorted world—one solely of polarity without enough duality to keep evolution moving forward.

So in relation to Masculine and Feminine Polarity Work, we use a richer framework designed to inspire the mind to find its own answers to the nature of reality. We can see dark feminine energy as being in the realms of divination, asking for help, tuning into energies and entities of a higher consciousness that are not part of our soul or higher self, channelling information in the occult, in reading cards, in charging crystals with information, in healing through the death of something old. She is sex magic the material, the creation of desire. She is the burning of sage, the blessing of water, and many other activities which many Western modern hippies and yoga lovers are doing in high street studios.

And dark masculine energy can be seen as our inner warrior, the part of us that can walk through hell with a smile on our face, willing and able to enforce our will onto the world, to create, to be brave, to have an ego, to say I AM, and that I AM part of God's divine plan.

The dark is exciting, a little dangerous, and essential for life.

Light feminine is much more accepting, she is, the going with the flow, dancing with life, seducing life, being magnetic, and drawing to her all she needs simply by looking within herself instead of without.

Light masculine energy is our connection to source, to God, to total oneness, with no distortion, no agenda, or imposition of our free will onto others, or the will of others onto us. No matter how light or of good intention, his will is solely with source, his interpretation of God.

No one perspective of seeing the world is correct, we need many perspectives to exist in a multi-dimensional reality, to be happy, and to keep evolution moving forward.

The dark and light, masculine and feminine, are not a focal point of this framework, but you are free to bring in and incorporate these additional perspectives with the framework as you see fit. It can be especially helpful during shadow work, to emphasize the positive within our darkness.

Any one model that claims to flawlessly explain the whole of reality is a trap, as the whole of reality cannot be explained without contradiction, as contradiction is fundamental to the nature of reality.

36
Making Our Desires Healthy

The purpose of using the polarity framework is *not* to always be in our mature, but to make both our immature and mature *healthy*. When we don't have physical, mental, and emotional alignment around a certain issue, it's hard for us to know what we really want in life and we stay trapped in our mind, rejecting what we don't want *(but still desire)*. Because we suppress our desires, they become unhealthy and the only way for us to find out what they are trying to teach us, is to give them space, allowing them to transform. Try the following:

1 Write down all the suppressed and unhealthy desires that come to your mind right now; they might be violent, selfish, sexual, or even scare you. You don't have to share them with anyone else and some you might not even want to write down, but the important point is that we are being honest enough with ourselves to find the connected issues that they represent.

2 Next, find the common issue, theme, or thread in these desires and then share these with a friend, therapist, or your partner, if you're doing this exercise together. You can share as much or as little as you like about your answers from question one.

3 Now put the common thread, or threads onto the polarity framework, see what it looks like, including your shadow. Use the standard process;
   – Embody the opposing mature.
   – Evolve into the mature of that same polarity.
   – Avoid the opposing immature or a process of your own.

4 Identify *and write down* the next steps that you will take to:
   – accept these unhealthy parts of yourself and give them space so that they can transform into . . . *(insert your written positive statement and intention here)* . . . it's important to *roughly* know what we want them to transform into, but allowing this to change as we understand ourselves more.

– make these parts healthy. Write a list of positive, specific, and measurable actions that you can hold yourself accountable for.

Don't feel too committed to anything that you write down, often transforming our shadow and unhealthy desires is a process, so we need to go part of the way through it before we really understand why we do what we do and what it is that we really want.

Example of personal shadow work

Occasionally when I see unconscious behaviours, especially within consumer and capitalistic trends removed from nature, destroying our planet and causing suffering, I can feel violent and want to lash out and hurt people for their unconscious behaviours, to teach them a lesson from my immature. I go into my shadow of violence and dominance from fear and lack of trust.

The polarity framework teaches me that I need to be more devoted to my own masculinity, my own values and my own leadership. To trust my mature masculine impulses more and to hold my boundaries better. Trusting that when I express myself like this I need less violence, less dominance and less control over others as the people around me evolve and make better choices when I express myself without violence.

Part 4

THE PHYSICAL, MENTAL, AND EMOTIONAL BODIES

37
Dimensions of Consciousness

~

Different people and schools describe dimensions in different ways. In this book, we apply a physics perspective to the dimensions: 3D, 4D, and 5D. More esoteric perspectives show twelve dimensions of consciousness, acting as a continuous cycle of separation, leading back to oneness. Quantum physics has similar descriptions, but in practical day-to-day terms it's much easier to work with three:

- Our physical body is 3rd-dimensional = always in the present moment.
- Our mental body is of the 4th-dimension = in linear time.
- And our emotional body is 5th-dimensional = beyond space and time.

As we understand reality through dimensions, the most important thing to remember is that each one of us is the centre and creator of our own universe, inviting in the consciousness of others and their personal universe to our own, to inspire and learn from each other. Creating a relationship with another is like creating a shared universe, a shared playing field. We can never totally understand someone, because to us, in our universe, they can only be a mirror for ourselves. So, any judgements we take on towards them, following the laws of attraction and resistance, have to also be judgements onto ourselves.

No matter how far we feel we have evolved or expanded our consciousness, all of our experiences and perspectives come back to and are translated with our linear 4D understanding—our understanding of time, totally governed and ruled by the laws of polarity and duality, attraction and vibration.

Parallel to our 4th-dimensional reality, is our dream world and the astral world. Linear time, as a 4th-dimensional concept is of the mind. Time is real, because the mind is real; we need a linear reference to experience reality, but it is only a partial truth. In the same way that our dreams are real because our mind is real, our mind makes up our dreams in a similar way to how it makes up our experience of time. The difference between the astral and the dream world is that:

161

- Our dreams come from our own life experience and are an expression of our separate self. When we dream, we are locked in separation and limited by our own life experiences, what our mind knows and understands through our personal history.
- The astral (the upper astral and the lower astral) is like dreaming with the collective consciousness; we are not alone in the astral and our experiences are not only shaped by our mind, but by our fully integrated self, as it expresses in relation to others.

The more of an emotional understanding of reality we have, the more of a 5th-dimensional understanding we have. For most people, the more alignment we have between our physical, mental, and emotional bodies means the more lucid we can become in our dreams and in the astral (when we apply the effort and discipline needed).

A fundamental difference between various esoteric paths is that they will either try to "transcend" the illusion, moving back to a place of oneness, back to being at one with God or aspire to physically "wake up in the illusion", to become conscious of all that is from a sense of separate self. These schools believe that if we wake up in the illusion, as we do when we dream lucidly, we will have the power to create and shape waking reality in the same way that we create and shape our dreams. Waking up in the illusion is fundamental to authentic Tantric paths, and is one reason why they put greater focus on pleasure and enjoying life, as they are not trying to leave this plane of existence, but to experience 5th-dimensional consciousness in it.

38
De-armouring the Three Main Bodies

We all have lots of bodies. Our physical body is the highest density of light. This is why we appear solid, although really, we are vibrating light reflecting molecules (or light generating molecules depending on your belief system).

Then we have our etheric field, which in its lower levels of abstraction, is an electromagnetic field (EMF). Plants have one, animals have one, trees have one, as does anything that runs on an electrical current, from computers and mobile phones, down to the wiring in a house. We can use our etheric field (our electromagnetic field) to bring chi, prana and life force into our bodies. It is also what animates us. If we look into the mirror *and we're happy, we generally look good.* This is partially because we are all viewing physical matter through our own etheric field. A malleable layer of light. And since matter is vibrating molecules of light, it means that matter is malleable, our face is slightly malleable.

The more alignment that we have between our physical, mental, and emotional bodies, the more power we have to work with light to change our physical reality, as well as our emotional and mental one. The essence of healing is to work with light.

What stops us having alignment, what stops us having power, is fear and trauma in our body. A heavy or denser vibration, one to do harm to others or to do harm to ourselves, blocks us from our power. This misalignment, between our three bodies is our safety switch:

- our physical body is 3rd-dimensional = always in the present moment;
- our mental body is of the 4th dimension = in linear time;
- our emotional body is 5th-dimensional = beyond space and time.

Our three bodies can often find it hard to communicate and understand each other because they work in three different dimensions, with each body having its own way of creating blocks, these blocks are our armour so when something hurts us, we remember it, so it cannot hurt us again. This was previously discussed in the chapter, *Surrender, Trust, Power, and Forgiveness,* in the section *De-armouring our heart,* where we looked at practical examples of how physical, mental, and emotional pain can all trigger each other to create physical, mental, and emotional reactions.

As the physical body is the highest density of light, the densest, all of our painful and traumatic memories are stored in our physical body and create armour so the same pains cannot hurt us again. Unfortunately, as we live in a vibrational universe, instead of protecting us from our pain, our emotional and physical armour simply attracts more pain into our life. Even after working with our emotional and mental bodies, forgiving ourselves and others, if we are not also working with the physical body, our trauma is likely to come back or never fully heal, so we will not find our full alignment or our power, unless we work holistically.

De-armouring is discussed further and in more practical terms, in the Integrative Healing section of this book.

39
Unlocking Conscious Awareness from Our Mind and Developing Emotional Awareness in Our Glands

What we are is conscious awareness, but the majority of us lock conscious awareness into the mind. When we are asked, *"Where are you?"* most of us will point to our mind and say, *"I am here."* We lock conscious awareness into our mind through the relationship with our breath, by creating a short and shallow breathing rhythm with lots of pauses. The pause is where we think, so by having this short and shallow breathing rhythm, it means we spend most of our life *"thinking"*.

You might have noticed if you're doing something complicated, that you stop breathing, until you finish your thought. This is because it is difficult to have conscious awareness in the physical and mental bodies at the same time. They are two different bodies. It's not impossible, but without alignment, physical, mental and emotional alignment, having conscious awareness in more than one place is difficult. The short and shallow breathing rhythm means that we no longer have an authentic relationship with our breath, our physical body or our emotional body.

We cut ourselves off from communicating with the innate wisdom and understanding that resides in our DNA and we stop ourselves from expanding our awareness and creating emotional intelligence.

Please note: *In yoga and spiritual practice, the pause in the breath is not normally thought or mental chatter, but connection to something more than ourselves and often explained as the transmutation and then sublimation of energy into our third eye, or pineal gland, taking us closer to transcendence.*

When we try to plan everything logically with our mind, we do not have alignment, as we are not listening to our physical or emotional bodies, so, we cannot have our true power. The unhealthy ego has taken over and locked us into our mind. Our perspective of the world is thus reduced and comes from separation, we forget that we are conscious awareness and start to believe that, *we are,* this sense of separate self that lives in the mind, reacting to the world from our memories, trauma, and programming.

Initially, this is needed, it is a process that happens to us as children so that we can form a healthy ego, a healthy sense of separate self. In our separated state, we might say that we are conscious of approximately 5 to 10% of who we are (non-scientific number). The other 90 to 95% is our subconscious mind, our inner masculine and feminine, our partner's inner masculine and feminine, our higher selves, the collective consciousness and the unconscious, the things we cannot understand because they are still unconscious. They are the unknown and yet to be discovered mysteries of the universe, which ultimately are the mysteries of ourselves.

To tap into more knowledge and to find understanding beyond our mind, we need to create physical, mental and emotional alignment, and to do this we have to learn how to feel more.

So many of us don't really feel our emotions because we have suppressed them. We've metaphorically and literally swallowed them down into our stomach. We've created a numbness inside and often don't breathe into our stomach, as that's where our pain is. Practical ways of working with the breath and to self-de-armour, create more emotional awareness and are central to using the integrative therapy practices within Masculine and Feminine Polarity Work.

Our stomach and our heart, each have more nerve receptors in them than our brain, these nerve receptors respond to electrical signals sent down by the brain through the central and peripheral nervous systems, powered by salts. The stomach, heart, and glands of the body respond and send electrical signals back up to the brain as feedback, but on higher levels of abstraction, everything is energy, energy is all around us and has information in it. Water is transformed on a structural level by etheric energy *(see Dr Masaru Emoto's research in his book* The Hidden Messages in Water*)*, and other objects store etheric information that we can read later. Crystals are very good receptors of etheric information, just as copper is for an electrical current. The nerve receptors in our stomach and womb, if you're a woman, also pick up etheric and emotional energy around us. When we can de-armour the body enough and change our relationship with our breath, we allow this information in.

Empathy does not start in the mind. Real empathy starts in the cells of our body, most often our stomach, with a relationship to our heart. This is why we have the common phrases, "listen to your gut", and "listen to your heart".

Notice, that if we sit next to an angry person for too long, we get angry, or how different environments affect us emotionally. The more we become aware of our emotions and that of others, the more obvious it is that we are conscious awareness. If we feel that we have too much empathy, then it is likely that we need to develop more mindfulness, being able to feel someone else but without getting lost in their story, making their mental pain and trauma our own. It is a process and skill that needs to be learned, with many of the key aspects covered in the integrative therapy practices of *de-armouring, breathwork, and energetic bodywork.*

Developing empathy, our emotional intelligence, alongside our intellectual intelligence with mindfulness and the ability to observe ourselves is crucial for our evolution and the evolution of humanity. We should aim to develop so much conscious awareness that we can simultaneously experience our emotions, use our intellect, and be mindful.

Our Mind Creates Emotions

Our mind creates emotions that are different to etheric emotional information coming in. When we have a memory, we create electrical signals that send information to our pituitary gland, thyroid gland, adrenal glands and all of the other elements and glands of the endocrine system, as well as the liver, which create chemicals. These chemicals: dopamine; serotonin; cortisol; and adrenalin, to name a few, create our emotional states. Emotional states that confirm to the mind that it is correct. This pattern, and these electrical signals, are then engrained into the brain. In some cases, it almost becomes an addiction and we, healthily or unhealthily, brainwash ourselves with emotional addictions, regardless of whether it is linked to substances or not. And because on this level our brain is only following a pattern of familiarity, we can become addicted to our sad and lower emotions, just as much as to our happy and high ones. Thus, experiencing empathy on the level of our glands and from our stomach, having emotional information that does not come from the mind as a logical thought process and set of judgements, is so valuable. It can help us evolve our understanding and our mind, as well as precepts of collective consciousness in where these emotions come from.

Transforming emotions in the body can help to release chi, prana, and life force. Chi *(Chinese)*, prana *(Hindi)*, and life force *(Western)* are three terms for the formation of energy on a quantum level. Each culture has given us a slightly different way to understand quantum energy; although it's useful to know them all in practical day-to-day terms, it is simpler to say that chi, prana, and life force are the same. For the majority of us, our most intense experiences of feeling this quantum energy in our body will have been related to our sexual experiences.

As discussed before, the first law of thermodynamics states that *in a closed or isolated system, energy cannot be created or destroyed, it can only transform.* So, when we are working with energy, the questions become:

- where are the boundaries and what defines our system as closed?
- how do we open a closed system?
- how do we work with open systems to create more energy?

From the highest 4th-dimensional perspective, we all take our energy from the sun and the stars in the night sky; the sun burns, trees grow, and life on Earth is sustained.

As a human being, we are a closed and isolated system, living in 4th-dimensional linear time. But this is only a partial truth. When we connect to another human being sexually, we transfer energy *(emotional, sexual, and etheric 5th-dimensional energy),* and it is through the merging of the masculine and feminine energies that we can create new life and new energy, that we can create a baby.

As discussed, emotional energy *(which is also sexual energy)* in the sense of empathy, is 5th-dimensional and etheric. Etheric energy is a higher abstraction of our electrical magnetic field, just like from a layman's perspective, cellular data technology is a higher abstraction of electrical energy, *they are both measurable frequencies.* It is hard to apply exact physics to 5th-dimensional energy or our etheric field, but when done correctly, instead of just moving around or burning up, old emotional energy, *which might be the right thing to do when there is a lot of trauma,* the transformation of emotions can open up our system, allowing new chi, prana, and life force into the body.

The transformation itself can create excess energy and lifts our vibration so we experience energy in a different way. The experience is of having more energy, because our emotional vibration is higher. Thus, we create 5th-dimensional energy that expands conscious awareness by:

- transmuting sexual energy, from our sexual organs and glands to our mind;

- transforming low, vibrating, dense emotional energy into higher vibrations.

How the energy in our physical and mental bodies is affected by our emotional well-being, beyond nutrition and getting enough sleep, is related to the amount of 5th-dimensional / emotional energy that we have access to on the 4th-dimensional plane. So, when we experience empathy and we are able to transmute and use our sexual energy for other purposes, we are no longer in a closed system, we are no longer bound by the laws of thermodynamics from the highest perspective of the sun, *and other stars in the night sky,* providing all of our energy.

In our daily life, by cycling through high and low, dense and light vibrations, by not always being "happy" and "positive", we are able to create potential for new emotional energy. Becoming more empathic and using our sexual energy is key to not being stuck in a closed system. When our vibration is higher, we are more capable of attracting chi, prana, and life force from outside of the physical self *(including natural elements such as: sun; earth; air; fire; water; metals, gases, and crystals, as well as generating it with our six senses),* because we moved from a vibration of fear into love. But, at different times of our life, we might experience this differently depending on our natural balance of dark and light at the time.

This process can feel really good, even if we're releasing anger, rage, and grief; these emotions are powerful and as they release, if we relax the body enough, the fascia unwinds and the parasympathetic nervous system also releases tension.

The mind is not always sending signals to the muscles, organs, and glands, saying shake and move. In some trauma work we might see this, but when more pleasurable and blissful experiences occur, such as an orgasm, where the body wants to move and express, it is because emotional energy is being transformed in the cells of our body. The kind of emotional energy stored in our glands is partly dictating how we feel and the type of person that we are.

People who feel cut off from their emotions may find it more difficult to move conscious awareness into their heart and sex, and surprisingly people who meditate a lot, developing incredible mindfulness, can sometimes also find it difficult to allow consciousness to reside in their sexual glands, especially when embracing sexuality is not part of their spiritual practice or culture. Meditation practices can help make us better people, but will not necessarily increase our emotional intelligence. We need to expand conscious awareness more, so that we can:

- think (intellectual intelligence);
- feel (emotional intelligence);
- and be mindful (observe), all at the same time.

Many non-dual practitioners risk suffering from depression when they only ever observe their feelings instead of feeling them. Eventually, our glands will stop communicating with us emotionally, because we have stopped listening. Then we only have access to emotions of the mind, we are cut off from our intuition and have less access to 5th-dimensional energy, thus are only associating with, or are locked into, our sense of separate self.

We expand our conscious awareness to this new place, where we can think, feel, and be all at the same time, by working with our trauma and our shadow, making our mature and immature desires and expressions healthy, as we align our three bodies.

Orgasms Change Our Vibration

Nearly every gland in the body is capable of some form of ejaculation and of releasing chemicals and hormones.

When we have an orgasm, every cell in our body vibrates and transforms, so in these moments it's good to be with somebody who loves and accepts us, appreciates us and has gratitude for us or that we have good intentions for ourselves, to give our own body its new vibration.

Our cells pick up and are etherically filled with the vibrations in our environment, often coming from our partner (again: please refer to the research of Dr Masaru Emoto in his book *The Hidden Messages in Water* for science that supports such claims). But sometimes love, acceptance, gratitude, and appreciation are not what we want, and we desire more polarity, darkness and rough sex. There is nothing wrong with this if it's what we want, but for a healthy life we need our lover to imprint higher vibrations into us during orgasm on a regular basis and more often than darker ones. When we don't have this, we need to learn to do it for ourselves, or if this is not yet achievable, to find other ways to meet similar needs, be it through affectionate times with friends, long hugs, or seeing a therapist, bodyworker, or healer, one who can hopefully guide us to a more sexually liberated and fulfilling relationship with ourselves, allowing us to change our own vibration through orgasm.

We are not designed to fix all of our problems and change our vibration with our mind. To do this, we would probably need to chase events back to our great-great-grandmother, and even then all we could do is forgive her. As human beings we are designed to release our trauma and change our vibration through pleasure. We need to forgive people for where we feel they wronged us and simply trust that as we do this, we change our vibration and the world becomes a nicer place. When people start to de-armour their bodies as part of a holistic and integrative practice, they change their vibration, hence pain and sadness is released and our vibration transforms.

The aim is to be in a place where we release and transform physical, mental and, emotional pain through pleasure.

40
Natural Polarity

For one person to be abundant, another does *not* need to live in lack, but when the immature masculine is in control, we will have a reality where the natural polarities of nature and universal law are suppressed.

In an immature masculine system, for one person to be abundant, another needs to live in lack.

The economy, time management and our current relationship to work and rest are not natural polarities. Natural systems show many models of interdependence and diversity, the flow of chaos and order, driving evolution forward.

Life is supposed to be abundant and in a mature masculine system, we would all live abundantly.

The animal kingdom has a lot of power-over systems within it, but less greed and stupidity. As sentient beings, our role is to evolve beyond both power-over systems and greed, along with many other unhealthy manifestations.

Both of the below statements have truth in them, although they conflict each other:

- the amount of pleasure we experience equates to the pain we have experienced (law of polarity);
- pain attracts pain, pleasure attracts pleasure (law of attraction).

Working with natural polarity often means balancing such conflicting truths.

When We Truly Forgive

When we truly forgive, we can find natural polarity on the mental, emotional, and physical levels again, we can move around the polarity framework with ease, releasing our reactive behaviours and embodying higher truths.

Forgiving our parental role models, means we can embody the archetypical *"mature"* mother and father, developing these mature and higher vibrational states as our own, without their trauma: re-parenting ourselves.

Changing pre-programmed behaviours passed down from generation to generation, helps us unlock conscious awareness from the mind, developing more emotional awareness and intelligence.

This in turn supports the awareness of how our main seven energy centres work with the physical glands of our body, allowing us to become more aligned and integrated each day.

Forgiveness is key to finding our way back to natural polarity, both individually and collectively.

41

Spectrum of Emotions and How to Raise Our Vibration

As discussed earlier, many emotions, qualities, attributes, virtues and traits have the same essence and are vibrating and being experienced on different levels. As we recognize these spectrums, our relationship to duality starts to transform. Discernment is a higher vibration of judgement, and knowing, a higher vibration of discernment. Suddenly we see that knowing, discernment, and judgement are all different expressions of the same theme.

An old Buddhist saying is, "The only thing in life you can rely on is that everything changes."

This is true because everything is energy and energy vibrates and transforms once it is fully experienced. So, in one sense, everything in life changes and in another, nothing in life ever really changes except for our vibration, not even time. To transform a situation from an unhealthy to a healthy one, we only need to change our vibration. We might need to change unjust acts and situations in the world too, or simpler things like our home or job, but unless we change our vibration, the injustice will return.

Ultimately, all emotions with a high vibrational frequency are an expression of love, and with a low vibrational frequency, an expression of fear (hate also exists in a relationship with love and fear, and this is covered later), but this level of understanding does not help us take action, so we need more levels of abstraction.

From one perspective, we might say that states of grace, flow, and peace vibrate higher than love. This is another useful perspective for us to use as we integrate more multiple polarities and truths into our being. But to understand polarity using love as an expression of oneness is the most helpful.

When we look at our major emotions on this spectrum, with a non-dual perspective, it's easier for us to see and understand that most things in polarity to one another are actually one and the same, they are of the same energy. As the laws of physics teach us: energy can never stay the same, it can only transform. So, when we fully experience something, an emotion or an energy, it has to change, it has to transform:

If we are happy and we fully experience our happiness, we cannot be happy any more, the vibration has to increase to a higher level. Happiness turns into joy, joy turns into bliss, and bliss into greater bliss. This range, scale, and spectrum of emotions just keeps increasing until eventually we reach the experience of Nirvana. But in the same way, if we don't fully experience our happiness, we can get sad. And if we don't experience our sadness, we can become depressed, and then more depressed, until we hit rock bottom. By not accepting and fully experiencing our emotions, we lower our vibration. We become denser, we "feel" heavy, and we have less light in our cells.

The other thing that many people experience is getting stuck, we reject our pain and at the same time we hold on to our pleasure. My country, my football club, my favourite jacket, my favourite seat, my, my, my . . . When we do this, we cannot grow and we cannot change. We bounce around a very limited scale of emotions, a little happy, a little sad, but never truly authentic. To experience our greatest pleasures and joys in life, to raise our vibration, we have to fully accept everything in life without attachment. This is the mature feminine, totally loving and accepting of our joy as much as our pain, our anger, our jealousy, our heartbreak, our loneliness, our aggression, and whatever else it is that we feel. The feminine knows that our pain leads to and creates some of the deepest and most beautiful moments of our life, so she has no need to judge it. She loves and accepts all of the things that we are ashamed of or feel guilty for, unconditionally. Our quickest way back to happiness and joy, is to feel all of our feelings, no matter how painful. *The path to bliss is to not be attached to our pleasure and to not be scared of and reject our pain.*

Take a moment to imagine a world where everybody has a higher vibration, it does not mean that bad things will never happen again (they probably will), but our experience of them will be drastically different. Eventually, as we change our relationship to judgement, to pleasure and pain, to good and bad, then having a good cry and feeling our negative, lower vibrational emotions can actually be pleasurable.

The fundamental key to raising our vibration in daily life is the demonstration of non-judgment through:

- non-resistance
- and non-attachment.

But this is only possible when we have a healthy mature masculine, who holds boundaries, space, and keeps us safe, which is mostly done through non-action: just knowing, being, and holding the energy of the mature masculine is enough.

Attraction, Resistance, and Attachment

When we look at the concept of resistance and attraction on a polarity spectrum, we again see that they are the same thing, just vibrating on different frequencies. By resisting something, we must at some level also be attracting it, because the more we resist it, the more we focus on it, the more likely it is to show up in our life. When we resist something, it is a sign that we are pushing it into our shadow, either because we are afraid of it, ashamed of it or because that's what we already are and cannot accept it. Whether this is because of guilt, shame, the need for approval, or something else, *often the reason is not as important as exploring our resistance.* Once we explore our resistance to something, accept it and experience it, we can release whatever it was that we were originally resisting.

Positive affirmations are great and it really is very important to be positive, but unless we can be authentic, we are lying to ourselves. Some change and transformation can happen through such affirmations, but inauthenticity stops us from living our full potential. Fake positive affirmations come with a polarity all of their own and we need to be aware of this. Experiencing our negative emotions without attachment, allows them to transform to higher vibrations. This is true for many qualities and virtues, some examples include:

- inhumanity > sympathy > compassion
- condemnation > rejection > neutrality > acceptance
- resistance > neutrality > attraction
- depression > sadness > happiness > joy
- judgement > discernment > knowing

So, by not being attached to our inhumanity and condemnation of ourselves and others, our resistance, depression and judgements, means that we can move to experiencing more of the positive expressions of each spectrum. We can also see how the opposing traits on the Polarity Framework all relate to each other and can be viewed as a polarity spectrum, thus of the same energy:

- attention seeking > arrogance > humbleness > self-assurance
- attachment > ownership > interdependence > diversity
- blaming > shaming > honouring > empathy
- manipulation > domination > worship > devotion
- overly emotional > overly intellectual > emotionally and mentally balanced > intuitive
- passive-aggressive/jealous > competitive > selfless > accepting
- victimhood > judgementalness > discernment > creative
- anxious > avoidant > responsibilities/boundaries > freedom/trust

So, by taking away our resistance or attachment to feeling the lower vibrational energies and emotions, means we are able to feel the higher and mature ones.

Language is simply a tool to express our creativity in duality. We should each find the words that work best for us in the framework, if some don't fit, don't use them. Whenever we focus on one quadrant of the Masculine and Feminine Polarity Framework, we should always be conscious of the other three. The listed traits on the framework are not exhaustive or definitive, the framework should always be left open for interpretation, using alternative traits that fit our situation and personal use of language the best. Knowing that, *"no matter where we are on the maps, we will always be all things, related to all expressions"*, is really helpful in understanding ourselves as a whole being. Even if we are resisting certain things, we can see how they are a driving force in our life with our fear of them, meaning they have power over us or more accurately, our fear of them means we block ourselves from our power.

When we are more familiar with just having masculine or just having feminine expressions, then by acknowledging and seeing how the traits are the same, just vibrating differently, we are able to integrate the masculine and feminine poles within ourselves much faster.

When we experience someone blaming or manipulating, instead of labelling them as this, pushing them into greater identification with it and making us the opposite, we can simply start to acknowledge that this person really needs more of the mature principles in their life, they simply don't have enough access to their maturity because they have too much fear. By seeing ourselves as whole and complete people, and others in this way too, we no longer need to identify with one thing and fight the other. We can just see we are all variations of something, in any moment:

- A % of healthy mature masculine;
- A % of unhealthy mature masculine;
- A % of healthy mature feminine;
- A % of unhealthy mature feminine;
- A % of unhealthy immature feminine;
- A % of healthy immature masculine;
- A % of unhealthy immature masculine;
- A % of healthy immature feminine;
- A % of masculine shadow;
- A % of feminine shadow.

For each experience we could break it down even further into the framework, for example:

- A % of anxious;
- A % of avoidant;
- A % of responsibilities and boundaries;
- A % of freedom and trust.

The exercise is *not* to assign numbers to any of the above, everything is in flux and change. We could look at each trait as being a singular moment, and each moment as being a playing piece on a huge, ever-changing 5th-dimensional chessboard.

Trying to calculate all potential moves and outcomes, like we do on a two-dimensional chess board, is useless. The negative and painful actions on one level are creating the most joy and learning on another.

The moment we start enjoying the game and are able to look to universal laws to evolve our experience, is the moment we start winning.

As we unlock new levels of reality by lifting our vibration and realizing the game is one of interdependence and co-operation, life starts to make sense.

42

The Actual Root Cause
of Our Problems

Most of our reactive behaviours, unhealthy parts of our ego, and mental and emotional blocks come from traumas and events in our life leading up to the age of around eight. A pattern is created that replays throughout our life until we solve and heal the traumas, thus creating a new programme for our mind. *But,* when we look for the root cause of our problems, it's not normally the actual trauma that happened to us, but what this trauma or life event has to teach us.

The root cause for most of our problems is the lesson we need to learn.

Solving all of our blocks and healing all traumas in the body is not a wise thing to do if we are not learning from them. We may start to live a life free of pain and trauma, but for our own evolutionary path, we have taken our potential away.

Your pain is expensive, so please don't waste it.

When working with pain and trauma in our three bodies, it is important to check that we are healing holistically:

- If the mind has already solved the problem, healed, forgiven, and integrated the lesson, then it really is okay to clear the trauma in the physical and emotional bodies. We might have solved our problem or trauma years ago and learned the lesson, but never found a way to release and transform it in the body, so we never fully healed.
- If the trauma is so big in the body that it's almost paralyzing, then it's best we see a trauma therapist and/or a bodyworker. They can help us alleviate the biggest pains, so that we might then be able to start work in a more integrative way, possibly using the Masculine and Feminine Polarity Framework to help us identify what our lessons are.
- Often the process of working with the body, reveals the trauma and the lesson, so there is no set or right way to work. We just need to ensure that we develop our physical, mental, and emotional bodies as we go.

Once we've learned from and healed our trauma or past events, sometimes we might still need reminding of the lesson, so our subconscious mind recreates the trauma. And we keep relearning the same lesson, over and over again until it's fully integrated, with nothing left to teach us.

Old traumas resurfacing are metaphors of the soul. If the same issue comes up over and over again, instead of looking at the story connected to it, we can look at what is this re-occurring trauma trying to teach us? Often, it's better to be met with our same old demons over and over again, opposed to creating new traumas and tragedies in our life so we can learn new lessons.

In some cases, this can take a lifetime, so it's incredibly important to understand what the lesson or *theme* of this repetitive trauma is. When we understand that our subconscious mind is doing this because from a higher perspective, *one that we can find hard to grasp,* we have decided that we need to keep being reminded of this lesson, until there is no doubt left that we are safe from it, it becomes much easier for us to accept a trauma or negative theme in our life because we are seeing it as a warning sign instead of a failure, or even as the polarity, tension or conflict that we need in life to ensure we have *balance* and *passion* to create life with. When we do this, our self-hatred and self-judgements are less and we can learn our lessons much quicker. Each time we accept and embrace our problems and lessons with gratitude and less judgement, the deeper our learning is and the quicker we move through our pain.

Repetition

To change our vibration, we need our mind to support us, and this comes with repetition, so if we have taken an unhealthy and negative vibration out of the physical and emotional bodies, we have to change the mental programme that supports it:

- Learning our lesson is key.
- But so is repetition. We need to repeat an authentic positive affirmation that reflects what we learned and our new vibration. But we also need to avoid lying to ourselves. Instead, we should work with the polarity framework until the affirmation feels true.
- Changing things in our day-to-day life and environment, supports us to remember that we've changed:
  - buying a new picture for the home;

 – moving some furniture or kitchen utilities;
 – adding something to our exercise routine;
 – or keeping a journal and starting a gratitude practice
will help us remember that we have moved from our old unhealthy behaviours. Each time we cannot find the salt pot, because we moved it to a new place in the kitchen, we are reminded and can repeat the affirmation that we *"love and accept ourselves"*.

We have to do things that help our mind remember and reaffirm that we have:

• learned a valuable lesson in life and changed our vibration;
• changed our mental programme and unhealthy reactive behaviours in order for changes to last.

43

Your Relationship as
Its Own Conscious Entity

There is you, with your expressions of masculinity and femininity, and your partner with their expressions of masculinity and femininity, and then there is your relationship, that also has its own expressions of masculinity and femininity.

- Applying the perspective of "relationships being conscious entities", helps us to not lose our self. When our relationships are their own conscious entities; with their own purpose; lessons to learn, and lessons to teach, it is much easier for us to learn from relationships and not lose our identity to them, thus keeping our individuality. Keeping our individuality generally means we will:
- keep passion alive;
- be able to be fully present with the other person;
- and, be clearer on our commitments.

It can be helpful to bring this concept to our partner, referring to the relationship, as if it was a person or child, asking questions like:

- is this good for our relationship?
- what is our relationship teaching us?
- how do we want our relationship to grow?
- what is nourishing in our relationship and how can it be more nourishing?

By creating more separation between our self and the relationship, it becomes much clearer to see what we as individuals bring, *what our masculine and what our feminine brings,* and what we want to receive, bringing us closer to our partner, because giving and receiving creates excitement on both sides.

In a healthy relationship, our differences complement each other, without forcing us to change or sacrifice a part of ourselves. Sacrificing who we are in a relationship for most people means to become similar to our partner, seeing the world and acting in the same way, so eventually polarity dies and so does the fire and passion.

In polyamorous settings, *seeing each relationship as conscious entities* with its own:

- form of consciousness;
- purpose;
- and lessons to learn and teach

is a good perspective to apply, because asking the question: *"How does the relationship with (partner A), affect the relationship with (partner B)?"* can create very different answers to, *"How does the relationship with (partner A), affect (partner B)?",* because we depersonalized it, so are less likely to move into unhealthy immature reactions.

When we start applying this concept to all of our relations: friends, family, and co-workers, we will generally be really surprised as to how dramatic the results are, especially when applied into business, organizational structure, and strategy meetings. But in relation to our inner masculine and feminine, the greatest learnings come from our intimate and sexual partnerships.

44

Working with the
Collective Consciousness

~

Depression is Political

When we are mainly acting from our unhealthy ego, the constant act of rejecting pain and chasing pleasure keeps us in our immature and unable to find a deeper meaning and understandings of life. We cannot realize or self-actualize, as we are too busy suffering or trying to avoid suffering. There might be amazing gym workouts, walks, and activities in nature, meditation sits, yoga classes and other momentary senses of peace, but we cannot find lasting peace and serenity because of constant reactions in our subconscious, created by unresolved trauma.

When a person transforms fears and releases attachments, a sense of joy from being alive is found, but sometimes there can also be a deep sadness. A sadness that comes from glimpsing a higher truth, knowing that we create our own reality, but not knowing what to do about it or how to change. For some people, this is the root of depression.

Evolving to find that life feels empty, pointless, and meaningless, no matter what meaning our immature self tries to give it, we can be left feeling depressed. We need more knowledge, higher truths, and understanding of universal law, so that we can integrate these into our life, working with the polarity, that they create.

Trust, Freedom, Serenity, Peacefulness, and Gracefulness, in the mature feminine can all easily devolve into feeling like a victim, but also devolve into depression. Like love, compassion, joy, happiness, sadness, anger, and laughter, depression is part of an emotional spectrum that exists in both the masculine and the feminine.

Depression is more common in richer, technologically advanced societies, where people have free time and safety and therefore can afford the luxury of being depressed (scavenging for food, avoiding starvation, or living in a war zone, does not leave much time to be depressed). When we re-frame depression as an evolutionary step, but a step in an "unhealthy" direction because we cannot integrate beauty or have what we want in life,

184

then we can look to the Masculine and Feminine Polarity Framework to help us move back into balance.

Depression is increased by frustration and a sense of meaninglessness that is propagated by our society, including governments; mainstream media; and the education system, but the reality that these institutions create is not "the" truth. We can only live in a reality inflicted upon us by these institutions when we choose to believe in them. Taking this to the extreme of being locked in a prison cell makes this concept hard to grasp, but the concept of prison and punishment are of the immature masculine and currently, it is near impossible, for most, to choose anything different. While we are working to evolve the immature masculine, we need to live in and abide by its rules and structures, but when the mature masculine is strong and prominent, these structures will change:

- working hours;
- the daily commute;
- a religion we don't fully accept, but practise;
- rules and bureaucracy designed to keep people busy, doing useless activities so that they cannot expand their consciousness;
- or whatever else it is that we feel imprisoned by.

Using the reflective nature of the universe is the only way we can truly evolve our imprisoning structures and thus our depression.

Attachment to What Is

One of the main reasons that the mature masculine is not here, is our *"attachment to"*, or at least *"fear of"*, changing these structures and systems. It can seem impossible to even think that we can move away from existing systems and change how society works, so our development work has to start on the personal level.

It's our own fear of the unknown and fear of not being in control that stops societal changes, more so than governments, thus stepping into our mature masculine and taking responsibility for the corruption in government, is the only way corruption in governments will stop. In a truly democratic society, the government is a reflection of the demos of the people. The crux of the problem in enabling enough mature masculine people (men and women) into power who are willing to fight on a political stage—a mostly immature political stage—is that people who act predominately from their healthy mature will not generally sacrifice their integrity in the way current politics requires. Thus in playing the game of politics to make it mature they are likely to become immature. Thus the transition takes time, but it is happening.

When we as a collective are ready to accept the radical changes that the mature masculine brings, he will be more present within us. We will align ourselves more to this mature masculine energy, and as we change, the world changes with us, creating the health and balance that is currently missing from our societies.

Including What We Want to Reject

Having the collective consciousness evolve with us should not *"just"* be preaching to the converted. Working and socializing with people who vibrate on a similar frequency and have similar views to us has merit in that we find the motivation and inspiration that we need to reach our goals and we take our "group", our mini collective-consciousness, further down our shared path. A lot like art and music, often called *"luxuries"*, walking this shared path brings pleasure and satisfaction, and developing in these areas is actually essential if we are to evolve consciousness.

We need to invest in higher levels of abstraction without guilt and in a way that helps the people starving, living in poverty and war to move forward and give hope, so that they can see what they will do with peace and freedom when they have it.

When we look at major 50/50 splits in democratic countries, it's because more cohesion is needed through conversations that create mutual under-standing, respect, and compassion. In a good democratic system, we would rarely vote on two polarized options and never when close to a 50/50 split, we would be looking at how to integrate the best of multiple options in a way that has the maximum benefit and makes the maximum amount of people happy, similar to how businesses work towards strategies, and fami-lies get over harder times. Taking half the population and saying, *"you're wrong, you're bad, your side just lost"*, is quite absurd.

Current political models are designed to keep us arguing about the best way to do something wrong, opposed to finding the best way to do something "well".

Many, many people are stuck in the same way of being and have been for years, while others seem to feel the cutting edge of four or five paradigm shifts all at the same time. It's often more fun to evolve higher, with like-minded people than to include the different vibrations of other people from unlike-minded groups, communities and sets of mini collective consciousnesses.

We always have free will, sometimes it's good to open up to more diversity *(mature feminine)*, and sometimes it's better to work more with our boundaries and interdependence *(mature masculine)*. On a global scale, we need this shift and we need more cohesion in personal transformation so that we are able to create planetary transformation. Simply forcing people to open up and include more diversity does not work, and is likely to push them further into their immature. A democratic vote with a predominantly immature demos (populace), will create immature decisions.

The foundation of leadership, from the mature masculine, is about helping others to evolve. Any government who does not have this as its premise, does not deserve power.

Global problems are complex and of course basic needs must be met before people feel that they are able to give. But when basic needs are met, the immature *will still act selfishly* from fear, lack and the shadow of greed, whereas the mature knows that selflessness and generous behaviour will create joy and abundance for all. A global value-based evolution of the mature masculine and feminine is needed, one that supports creativity, art, music, technology and a spiritual deepening, while also generating new directions for collective and individual growth. But without enough cohesion and shared direction of values, the majority of humanity and therefore the global collective consciousness becomes stuck. Power struggles and wars from the immature self are much more likely to break out, devolving value systems and the global collective consciousness.

By living through inspiring and successful examples, and sharing these with society as a whole, society and the larger collective can transform in progressive ways:

- schools can evolve;
- healthcare can evolve;
- big Pharma ends;
- the business and corporate world evolves;
- the rehabilitation systems in prisons evolve;
- the concept of punishment itself transforms;
- the hours in our working week;
- the financial system;
- the economy, all evolve.

But they can only evolve with us and the greater whole. Our personal transformation has to happen first, but it needs to happen aligned to the planetary transformation that we each desire and want to create. Sometimes it hurts and is counter-intuitive, but as we include and accept the lower vibrations in ourselves, we allow for balanced transformation with more cohesion of the greater whole.

Some esoteric teachings will warn us away from trying to improve the world on a large scale or having any kind of outward focus. They will say that everything is perfect, everyone chooses their life and is living out their Karma. The mature masculine would say that he is everything and everyone. He is the collective consciousness and everything is a reflection of himself. He can only heal himself through the mature feminine through his reflection. As he heals himself, he heals his reflection, as his reflection heals, he heals the world. By loving the feminine within and all of femininity without, *collective Karma changes.*

It's only after we transform our world and create a new environment that humanity as a whole can move on to new lessons and develop new abilities within the physical, mental, and emotional bodies, realizing our shared Karma. If we do not, then we will continue to go over the same old lessons and patterns that we have done for the last few thousand years, and the old esoteric teachings will remain correct.

Sometimes including and being open to new groups of people and values can feel like a sacrifice, a sacrifice that we are not willing to make. When we are truly mature and can act with discernment, we can welcome, involve and accept people without losing ourselves, and often in doing so, learn more about ourselves. It's true that if we spend a lot of time with someone, they will affect who we are. But it's also true that those same people, those parts of our consciousness that we deny and reject, affect our environment, which also affects us. So, either way, we cannot escape, they are part of us and will have an influence over us, seen or unseen, consciously or unconsciously.

We need to find win-win scenarios from our healthy mature masculine, even when problems look so big that we want to turn the other way and not take responsibility for everything in our world. But when we do take responsibility and shift our attention to creating the win-win scenarios, we will find that situations change more quickly and the more of us who do this, the quicker everything changes.

When we see 50/50 splits in democratic countries, it means that the cultural values and evolutionary gap between different sub-groups of people is too big. It's not that people need to start devolving, but that they need to start helping the collective evolve, making their views more accessible in a mature way, *which is also the best way to sustain a level of higher awareness and vibration.* This is not trying to create a monoculture (culture needs diversity, the feminine), but we should all be moving in the general direction of more joy, creativity, inspiration, love and awareness.

Overcoming Depression

The universe works in a similar way to our emotional body. We are the centre of our own personal universe, co-creating reality with the collective consciousness that is a part of the greater multi-dimensional whole. This might sound overwhelming for some but when we work with our subconscious mind, *"acting as if"* the above statement was true, we can no longer be or feel like a victim. We no longer need to succumb to someone else's will as we realize that their will is just a reflection of our subconscious mind.

When we allow our mind to believe that we are the centre of our universe and everything apart from our sense of "I AM" is an illusion, then we are accepting that we create our own illusion, we create reality and we create the universe simply by being. By fully adapting to this view and wholeheartedly living as if we believed it, we can work with the mind in an integrative way. We are then able to evolve the polarities within ourselves, and outside of ourselves much faster.

So, if you are depressed and you struggle with manifestation and working with the law of attraction, then try working with this concept. It's not *the* truth, it's a partial truth. It's not an easy concept to grasp, so feel free to write it down and think it over for a while. In your own words is best, but if you're struggling to sum it up try:

Reality is multi-dimensional and I AM the centre of my own personal universe. I co-create reality with the collective consciousness.
or
I AM the centre of my personal universe, co-creating reality with the collective consciousness that is a part of the greater, multi-dimensional whole.

Depression is a "stuckness", it can often mean on one level, maybe even a subconscious level, we have realized a higher vibrational truth and this truth translated into our reality is depressing. Depression comes from not fully accepting our pain, from rejecting parts of our self, from judging too harshly or not feeling like we can deal with our pain, so suppressing it. We end up creating mental patterns for depression by repressing how we truly feel. We train our mind and bodies to create chemicals that support our feelings of depression, so we stay depressed, never really feeling our feelings or fully expressing the original emotions or trauma, connected to the experience that made us sad. We build stories onto stories about why we feel depressed and although we might resolve these with the mind, they are not our real reason for the depression, so we do not create lasting change.

Depression comes from unexpressed emotions and feelings.

Most often, these emotions and feelings come from lessons we still need to learn, *maybe we need to learn acceptance or forgiveness because of a broken heart, or death of a loved one, or maybe there is something to learn from our jealousy or our impatience.* These emotions are an opportunity for growth to create more depth in our mature and immature traits.

I urge you to start looking where you are acting from your immature self, and even your shadow, and find where you can evolve these traits. As you do this, you will:

- realize new truths that do not depress you;
- change your vibration;
- attract new people and emerging cultures into your life;
- gain new knowledge and find new things to get excited about.

You can take a fresh start in the game of life, learning how to create more depth and meaning in your daily experiences. To beat depression:

- accept what is;
- breathe into your belly and feel what the experience is and then allow it to change;
- create a sexual relationship with yourself between your inner masculine and inner feminine.

These are the fundamental concepts discussed later in the Integrative Healing section of this book.

45

The Essential Nature of Love, Fear, and Hate

From a high vibrational perspective, fear is the absence of love, but love can also be the polarity of hate. We often see this in passionate and sometimes violent marriages, where love and hate become the same thing. The couple swing between high emotional states and become addicted to these states so do not change. This polarity of love and hate is not false, it's just a lower vibrational understanding and experience that leaves us victim to and locked into a polarized existence. When we are locked into such polarized states, love can feel absent, faithless, graceless, and unsafe with no direction to move; when this happens, we can work with the Masculine and Feminine Polarity Framework to:

- turn our hate back into fear;
- turn our shadow back to the immature (a healthy immature and a healthy fear).

In a dualistic reality, the absence of love, the lower vibrational experience of fear, is important. Fear protects us, motivates us and makes us act in certain ways. It helps us to remember, respect, work in and sometimes enjoy being in physically dangerous situations. As we understand that fear is separation and by being fearful, we increase our individuality, we can also understand that in a sense, fear created duality. Fear created this reality that we all live in. A reality where we can experience separation but also beauty. It is a way for "oneness" to experience itself, but once we have this realization, separation does not end, our human experience does not end. Embodying the realization of what fear really is allows a new level of consciousness to emerge.

The realization that fear is the absence of love sets us free in the illusion, the illusion that we have been unconsciously creating for a very long time. We realize that everything is, or has the potential to be love.

Used wisely, our fear creates more depth within ourselves and more depth within the collective. This depth can be healthy or unhealthy, so this

191

is *not* an invitation for us to create as much pain and suffering as possible, *not* to create more darkness that we later turn into light, but an invitation to act correctly when pain and suffering arise, to see it for what it really is: a moment of separation; of fear, and an opportunity for depth, abundance, and greater awareness.

Fear Is Matter

From an emotional energetic perspective, at its most basic level, everything that is physical is matter and has been created through fear. If the molecules are dense enough to vibrate together, to create something solid, then the molecules vibrate on a dense level of light, so on the emotional level of polarity, we would have to call this fear. So, our bodies, our physical bodies, are made up of fear, pain and trauma, thousands of years of fear, pain, and trauma, it's what, and who we are *(this statement is from the emotional body's perspective of why and how light forms into matter, it is more of a metaphoric understanding, a partial truth, to help us understand duality: light within dark and dark within light. Think of the pain and suffering in child birth for most mothers and babies which results in the greatest gift, the gift of life)*, but once the vessel is made and the molecules vibrate together in such density that allow us this amazing and beautiful experience of "being living breathing matter", we are able to evolve our predominately emotional experience from fear to love, while still keeping physical form. The fundamental principle of evolution is to transcend and include so we can live in separation, in dualistic reality that has been built on thousands of years of more pain and fear than love.

Knowing that we are one and knowing that we are love, does not stop us experiencing oneness from our individual and separate state.

Working with Faith and Grace

Emotional states of being such as love, faith, grace, joy, and serenity hold the highest vibrational truths. They encompass many other emotions and bring us closer to oneness. The application of love in duality, where fear is present, can at times be just as destructive as it is creative. This is why it is helpful to work with other higher vibrational truths, such as faith and grace. Their meanings might change and develop for us individually, but generally speaking:

Faith goes beyond trust. Faith is trusting in the unknown, trusting that the unconscious will manifest into consciousness exactly as it needs to. Trusting that everything is working out perfectly, no matter how bad or painful something is in the present moment. The more we learn to trust this, the less pain we manifest into our present reality, simply because our vibrational frequency is of a higher match.

Grace is always there when we have alignment. Grace enables different actions and polarities to all be working, unfolding and flowing, gracefully and at the same time. When we have inner alignment between both our masculine and feminine polarities and our emotional, mental, and physical bodies, grace is much more likely to show up within our lives. When we don't have alignment, we might still recognize grace happening. The Christian phrase for this is, "by the grace of God", or "may God's grace be with you".

Both faith and grace help us integrate into one whole person much faster, as does joy and all other emotional states that lift our personal vibration.

46
A Path to Self-Love

The purpose of self-love is to love ourselves so that we can love others more.

It's really easy for someone to say, *"just love and accept yourself"*, but when we have pain, fear and trauma in the body, this can feel like the hardest thing to do in the world. Our unhealthy ego is basically trauma, most personalities are made from mini traumas. These traumas create reactive behaviours, as opposed to mindfulness and mindful actions. Maybe each time you're confronted with authority, you always play the victim or you ignore them, do it your own way and be the rebel or maybe you fight for dominance. Or each time you meet your partner's parents, maybe you make inappropriate jokes or you pay fake and superficial compliments. Driving your car in heavy traffic, your traumas can create road rage, a sense of urgency, leading us to run red lights and commit other dangerous acts when there is no real urgency.

As we remove our traumas through integrative therapy practices *(such as de-armouring, breathwork, and energetic bodywork), we have more access to our authentic self* and it's from this place that we can see:

- why we don't have enough compassion or patience;
- who we still need to forgive;
- why we don't forgive ourselves;
- and why we don't fully love and accept ourselves.

Our pain and our trauma is there to teach us, so if we have not learned from our pain, if we have not healed it holistically in all three of our main bodies, it's likely that the pain and trauma will come back until we have fully learned from it, integrated its lessons and no longer feel that the memory of it is protecting us from something. Without trauma in the body, we stop reacting from fear and we act from love. We act from our aligned and integrated self, from mindfulness and discernment, and from creativity and inspiration. The integrated expressions of our masculine and feminine. But even if we take all of the trauma out of our body and we live from our aligned and integrated self, self-love can still be hard to achieve.

We are not here on earth to be isolated; we are here to be with others and to share love with others. It's the polarity with another human being that often creates our desires and excitements. It's what creates conditional love for us to later develop and evolve into unconditional love. But until self-love is achieved, our love for others is incomplete, there is an element of neediness or fear that accompanies our love.

By consciously separating the masculine and feminine polarities within ourselves, self-love becomes obtainable, we can create active practices of being in and embodying our feminine. Taking care of ourselves after a hard day, running a bath and making the home look nice, not for ourselves, in the normal sense, but for our inner Masculine. And we can go out, buy flowers, fix the bed, or broken furniture, not for ourselves, but for our inner feminine, then we can take this practice into the bedroom, into how we touch, stroke, caress, and pleasure ourselves. Eventually, this relationship will become even subtler, unconsciously filtering in to how we talk with ourselves, both mentally and emotionally.

When stress takes over and we start acting from our sense of separate-self in a fear-driven, over-power environment, what we need is a soft voice in our head, our inner lover, telling us what we need and want to hear. We need the voice that says, *"I love you."* Or, we need the voice of our strong masculine or inner father, giving us motivation and helping us to act from just reasons and causes in order to create the desired results. We should always be looking for integration, in no way should this process make us feel schizophrenic. On the contrary, the process of polarizing thoughts and personality traits, to remove trauma, should heal us and support us to become more integrated, especially when coupled with integrative therapy practices.

We can never truly separate the masculine from the feminine, the inner mother from the inner father, as they are one. But it's through working with their differences, their conflicting inner truths and inner desires, that we become more whole. Healing our traumas while separating and reintegrating the masculine and feminine polarities within ourselves gives us the best chance of achieving self-love.

Our mature feminine is the part of ourselves that can love and accept us unconditionally; all the bad, shameful things that we've done, all the pain in our lives and the pain we have caused others, no matter what it is. Our mature feminine loves us no matter what, like one hopes a mother would love a newborn child. The feminine knows that pain and hardship in our life eventually creates beauty when managed correctly. She does not try to fix or take the pain away, as she knows our pain is often our greatest gift.

Our masculine cannot love and accept us unconditionally, the immature is judgemental and the mature masculine has wisdom and discernment, he is choosing the best actions available for our life in balance with the greater whole. His essence means that he cannot say yes to the things he does not deem as right, but on one level, he can and does love unconditionally, because he is integrated with the feminine, we are always both poles, never just one.

In our full expression of mature masculinity, we do not accept the pain and the evil in the world, as we are here to transform it.

We all need both parts. We need the part that loves and accepts life unconditionally, that allows pain and drama in and even gives space for evil to emerge, so it can heal and transform *(our feminine)* and we need the part that says *"no"*, the part that has strong boundaries and uses free will to create and express individuality, the unique I AMness of each of us *(our masculine)*.

One of the feminine's biggest lessons is that:

Love, conditional or unconditional, can be destructive.

This can be the love of an immature or even mature mother, this can be heartbreak or any painful situation that arises because intense feelings of love were involved (if you are of the mindset that humans should never suffer, then try to soften your perspective on suffering and ask yourself if you would be happier to not cry when family members and loved ones die? Our grief can heal us so it is unwise to suppress or deny it).

Equally, when the love of something or someone turns into an addiction, it can be very damaging. The feminine needs to accept this, accept that life is an unfolding story with twists and turns, and accept that her love can hurt and even be fatal, and then she needs to continue loving fully and completely, regardless of any potential consequences.

Loving Others

We can also break our own hearts when we start valuing someone else, more than we value ourselves, hoping that by giving them all of our love, we will in return get back what we need, what we are unable to give to ourselves. But in reality, this rarely works, polarity and duality do not work like this:

- by overly focusing on our love for someone else, we can forget about ourselves. We can accidentally become polarized, creating a low form of self-hate.
- loving someone more than we love ourselves can also create the belief that what we love is out there instead of inside. By not recognizing the other as a reflection of ourselves, we give our power away and lose, temporarily or permanently, the parts of ourselves that we value the most.
- when a person we love leaves, if we projected everything that we loved about our inner masculine or feminine onto them, when they leave, we can feel that they took what we love about ourselves with them.
- our love for someone else can turn into an unhealthy addiction, meaning that we create a lack of self-worth by being overly identified with their self-worth, and we become addicted to both loving them and hating ourselves.

The good news is, when we realize that all the love that we project onto someone else, be it our partner or a crazy infatuation with a pop/rock star, celebrity, guru, or God, in a religious sense, is actually the love that we have for our own inner masculine as a woman, or inner feminine as a man, our life changes. We can use mind plasticity techniques and meditative practices to consciously transfer these feelings back to ourselves, which is the essence of Eastern practices that worship deities. Using the masculine and feminine split within ourselves, and actually imagining another energetic being within us, who is also us, whom we send our feelings of love, of self-love to, is a very powerful practice.

When we are in a mutually loving partnership, the love we feel for ourselves, our inner masculine or feminine, is the same love that we feel for our partner and as one increases, they both increase.

The love that we have within, being reflected back to us, is the natural disposition of a human being and the basis of how we generate more love into the world. By understanding the dynamics of "not loving ourselves" or our partner "not" loving themselves, we gain perspective and compassion. In no way should this example make us feel bad for our self-love sending someone else into self-hate or broken heartedness, nor should it mean that we choose to love ourselves less. If we feel that our partner is starting to become polarized, then we know that the impulse to love them more could easily make the situation worse if we are not loving ourselves. And if we see that our partner is loving us too much but not themselves, we know what their important work is and it gives us vital information in how we can support them.

As we change our abstract beliefs on the cellular level: physically, mentally, and emotionally, our use of basic universal law changes and we are able to use these laws clearly, because we have inner alignment. The more we expand our awareness, and build a relationship with our own emotional body, the easier it becomes to simultaneously:

- be a vibrational match for what we want;
- work with polarity to also attract what we want through resistance.

Although this is basically magnetism, energy generating magnetism, emotionally it is overly simplified and it's better to see how the laws of attraction, and polarity and duality work together with our free will for what we choose and are guided to align to.

The purpose of self-love is to love ourselves, so that we can love others more.

47
Jealousy

Jealousy is a common theme that can cause a lot of internal blocks. When we want to become something or create something in the world, we manifest others into our life who are doing something similar; the more we think of and want something, the more we will see that thing in the world around us, because we live in a vibrational universe.

Looking at the polarity framework:

- the immature feminine is jealous and resentful (with a vengeful shadow);
- the mature feminine has compersion (compersion, in the urban dictionary, but not yet the Oxford, is defined as: "feeling joy for another's joy");
- the immature masculine is selfish (with an egocentric shadow);
- and the mature masculine is magnanimous and generous.

As the framework shows us, if we are feeling jealous, one of the best ways to stop this is simply by being generous. By being giving in other areas of our life, we step into our mature masculine and evolve our immature feminine and this eventually transforms our jealous feelings into compersion, into feeling joy for another person's joy and all of the other mature feminine attributes such as self-assurance, diversity, acceptance, serenity, and love, which helps us in removing the need for jealous feelings.

Self-development and self-acceptance work might need to come first, developing more safety before we get here, but in the end, this is the mark of overcoming jealousy and having a quick way to rise above it when new jealous feelings are generated.

If we are feeling selfish, finding where we can feel compassion will gradually remove our reactive, selfish thoughts and behaviours. This can be from seeing a toddler walk for the first time, or for our friend winning at sports. To feel genuine happiness for another's happiness is truly a beautiful thing. And this supports us to move into our mature masculine so we become generous and magnanimous. We naturally want to give as we see and experience the joy it brings to others, as our own joy. We start to realize, acknowledge, and act from our interconnectedness and selflessness. We apply our wisdom through concepts such as gratitude and we are able to encompass so much more of life when we experience other people's joy as our own.

Jealousy often stems from false and degrading beliefs that we hold about ourselves. Many feelings that we experience as negative are generally a lack of something else. Lack is just a lower vibration of the "thing" that we actually want. The truth is that life can have everything in abundance and we can still get our need for balance and lower vibrational energies met.

When we can change our mindset from:

"love is a finite resource" to *"love is infinite"*
and
"when I share love with someone, I have less love to give" to *"when I share love with someone, I have more love to give"*

we are giving ourselves the mental programming needed to move away from jealousy.

The Tamera Peace Research and Education Centre in Portugal, has written extensively about how we cannot have *"Peace on Earth"* until we have *"Peace in Love"*, and the ways that men and women need to heal the rift between the sexes in order to create this peace. Having a large focus on human sexuality some may find their practices controversial, but the core of what they teach has wisdom in it, which is applicable to all of us.

Once all of our basic needs are met, the most precious thing we have, from a 4th-dimensional perspective, is our time, which is also the most finite. We need to choose wisely in regards to where we spend our time and if we become jealous of where someone else spends their time, then often being generous with our time is the correct thing to do, but not always. Sometimes, we just need to focus on our own development, but in a selfless way, developing selflessness so that we can accept their choices (an alternative antidote for jealousy), and ultimately embody more of our mature traits so we attract a better match, someone who opposes and contradicts us on the polarity framework in all of the right ways.

48
Money
~

Money and jealousy share a similar vibration. Following the polarity framework, this means that money also vibrates with comperion and generosity, because it shares the positive attributes of jealousy. As previously discussed, the law of resistance can create a self-fulfilling prophecy, because we are focused on what we do not want. If we focus on saving money because we feel poor, then we risk creating *"poverty consciousness"* that traps us into negative, lower vibrational energies. This can be more difficult to change than all of the other polarities on the framework, because money is not a natural polarity, it is a man-made polarity.

When we work with money, we need to consciously work with the law of attraction. It's important to remember that our current economic system is a broken one, built on the immature values of the masculine, so money issues cannot give us an accurate representation of our manifestation skills. As an immature man-made system that does not fit correctly on the polarity framework, it does not follow universal and natural laws as a mature one would.

Money, on the polarity framework, looks very similar to jealousy.

- the immature feminine is lack (with a shadow of poverty and deprivation);
- the mature feminine is abundance;
- the immature masculine is selfish (with a shadow of greed);
- the mature masculine is giving.

But we can see on the physical and material plane that what the immature masculine needs to move from being "selfish" to "giving", is "abundance". But this is a material abundance, a material energy, it's not an emotional energy that we create from within. So, this means that the polarity framework can only work to evolve our immature masculine when we already have personal, material, and financial abundance. So, money is not a natural polarity and this means that the immature masculine, for many people, has become trapped in his thinking. The law of resistance is more prominent than the law of attraction. Due to greed and selfishness,

201

resources seem far more finite than they actually are, so the selfish and greedy, fear-driven nature of the immature increases, which means that it's even harder to move into the abundant and giving nature of our mature, so the feeling of lack prevails, fuelled by our own greed and selfishness.

It's not to say that this cannot change for us on an individual level, even if we do *not* start with financial abundance. Using the laws of polarity and attraction with our free will, we can create and change anything, but as our current economic system is not a natural polarity, it means evolving into a healthy expression of the mature and immature in relation to money, for the majority on the collective level can feel almost impossible.

If we personally have financial abundance, then we can put money onto the polarity framework and work with the laws of polarity and duality, balanced with the law of attraction, to help evolve ourselves and the whole, but the real challenge here is in noticing that, because money is *not* a natural polarity, it's very hard to work on the individual and collective levels at the same time. To give generously of our financial resources and still be financially abundant takes intelligence, as well as a system change. It's not impossible, but difficult. Whereas, to give generously of our love, wisdom, creativity, and all of the other mature traits, generally means that we will increase in these things and be more abundant in all of them.

It's not that money is bad, but that the economy is a broken, an unhealthy immature system that needs transforming, and it is our responsibility to transform it to a reflection of our mature masculine. The polarity framework does not give us answers of how to do something, but it does frame our problems in a way that we can see the natural polarities and dualities, finding our own ways to make all four quadrants healthy individually and collectively.

From an abstract perspective, money is energy; an energy which gives us the resources that we all need to live on a physical and material plane. As we find ways to make our use of finite resources seem infinite, we can:

- live from a sense of abundance;
- give generously;
- find healthy expressions of being selfish, like caring for ourselves more;
- find healthy ways to use the feelings of lack, such as by creating emotional resistance that we later transform into a different kind of energy, be it creative, sexual, or something else.

If we do find ourselves feeling jealous or resentful of others because we don't have enough money to do the things we would like to do, or because someone is not giving us the time that we wish for, it's helpful to remember that:

With natural polarities we can create natural happiness. So, we should invest our time, energy, and what money we do have into working with our existing, natural polarities.

Over time, and with enough dedication, we can make all of our relationships healthy. From here, we have a much better chance of creating our own financial wealth and abundance, if this is our true desire.

Also, as we increase our collective health on the polarity framework, mature masculine systems become much more viable on the societal and collective levels, because we are a vibrational match for them, so a system change must follow.

Law of Attraction and Capitalism

By focusing too much on the law of attraction on an individual level and not enough on polarity, on both an individual and collective level, *we have created unhealthy competition in our use of the law of attraction.*

Far too many people who understand and can use the law of attraction, are still working in soul-destroying jobs that are not aligned to who they are and due to lack of money, they're eating foods not right for them and relying on medical care that hurts them even though they have the knowledge and heart ready for a much more beautiful world.

This is *not* to say that using the law of attraction, to create a life of abundance does not work, it can and does, but we need to acknowledge that working with the law of attraction in our current models of society, means it comes with an underlying tone of competition, unhealthy competition. Metaphorically speaking, *competition is the pink elephant in the room* when we apply the law of attraction into a capitalistic system. If competition was not an unhealthy factor within our vibrational universe, thus our application of the law of attraction, then there simply would not be so much poverty and suffering in the world. Once we acknowledge this about the law of attraction and accept more polarity into our lives, finding creative abundant ways to work with our shadow and dark side, then we can start to work in a way that better supports the evolutionary shifts that our societies need to be getting ready for.

Many people wish to live and work in a way that allows them more time: time for themselves, for each other, for community, and family. Time to, breathe, stretch, be coached, taught, and to teach, and coach. When money is seen as an energy and valued more equally to emotional, creative, sexual, spiritual and other energies, then we will be much closer to creating this world.

Loneliness does not come from being alone, but in having gifts and love to share and no one to share them with. – Carl Jung (adapted)

49
Creating Balance in Duality

Most of us agree that life needs balance. It cannot all be happiness, joy, love, and high vibrational states. We need a level of duality and an understanding of lower vibrational states to make life flow in a synchronistic way, allowing us to accept even our pain with grace, but rarely do we consciously try to create these lower vibrational states. Most of us spend our lives avoiding them.

So, what do we really believe? Do we take the time to think this through?

Do we believe:

1 The world is just a terrible place full of "bad" things, so there is no need to consciously create inner balance in our lives and we only need to fight for the positive?

Or do we believe:

2 that there is some higher power, a God, or the fractal patterns of the Universe, making sure enough "bad" things happen in our life, thus life naturally balances itself out and we have no control over the situation and no free will?

One of the highest perspectives that we can attain, is that there is no good or bad, and we simply experience life without judgement. But for most us, believing this and practising it fully, are two different things, so we need balance.

Whilst most religions and a lot of scientists agree that our free will controls our actions, our subconscious mind knows that we need balance. Thus, many of our actions and behavioural patterns are subconscious and taken to create balance in our lives, and the less mindful we are, the more that this is true, or as Carl Jung said: *"Until you make the unconscious conscious, it will direct your life and you will call it fate."*

If our unhealthy ego is dominant in control, and with an overly positive outlook on life, then unless our subconscious mind has false grandiose self-beliefs, our subconscious mind will often be focused on the negative in order to balance us. It's not that our subconscious mind is negative, it is just in relationship with all of the other parts of our being, so motivating us with fear instead of love because there is too much unaddressed and suppressed fear in our body.

When our vibration is high, our life flows gracefully, synchronicity starts to happen; we see friends on the street, all the traffic lights are green, we arrive everywhere in perfect timing, fish jump in the air as we walk past, as we think of something we see it, when we have forgotten something and need reminding, helpful reminders appear. The feeling is of *"being at one"* and in harmony with our environment and the universe.

Paradoxically, the key to keeping our vibration high is not being attached to *"the high"*, but embracing *"the lower"* vibrations when they are there and finding as much joy and gratitude in these moments as possible. This still gives us the balance that we need in life; the balance is not one of happy and sad, the balance is one of high vibrational and low vibrational, *fortunately there is no universal law that stops us from enjoying both high and low vibrational states.*

The happiness, joy and gratitude that we feel in a situation, partly depends on our judgement towards it, regardless of our vibrational level or anything else that affects us.

Imagination

Some people say that our waking life, which is our experience of separate self, is an illusion, the Maya, a waking dream, with rules and structures. The more inner-power and self-knowledge that we cultivate in our life, the more we can influence, change and break the rules of the illusion that we are unconsciously creating in our waking life. And this may be true, but if we get hit by a truck, it still hurts, unlike in our sleeping dreams, so *fortunately* the correlation is not 100%, but mental fantasies in our waking life, although illusions, generated by our imagination, can be used to create more balance. Similarly, we can use hypnosis and NLP in a similar way, integrating our mental programming with our imagination to create real and drastic transformation in our life.

Equality Is a Judgement

Once our consciousness moves to a point where we do not need to judge as good and bad, and when we understand that our pain is often a gift filling a momentary need, it means we can experience our lower, negative, vibrational energy without judgement, knowing that what we are doing in one moment, might be creating lower denser, or higher lighter vibrational emotions in another. Singing in a high voice compared to singing in a low voice, it's not that one needs to be good or bad in a sense.

It's important not to get lost in the observer role. We need to be able to observe our emotions with mindfulness, while on one level still experiencing them. Emotions are powerful and valuable, they, along with our free will and connection to higher levels of consciousness are what stop us from being organic robots with artificial intelligence and a limited lifespan. Especially our etheric emotions, which we experience through empathy and other means, opposed to emotions created by our mind with electrical control of our glands, that easily fit into binary code because they are generated from our sense of separate self. The observer role allows us to see the relationships between our own physical, mental, emotional, and spiritual bodies *and that of other people's* physical, mental, emotional, and spiritual bodies, and how they communicate without hierarchy, but with trust.

It is this trust, trust in whole integrated people, that allows us to move from the mind into the heart and the gut, knowing that these people, the ones our heart and gut have chosen to trust, will always fight for our survival and that of the ones they love on every level: physically, mentally, emotionally, and spiritually.

A lot of people use mindfulness in a way that cuts them off from their emotional intelligence, or they turn emotions and feelings into thoughts. I need this emotion to have a, b, and c, in my life, but then we don't have the emotion, we only have thought. To observe and experience at the same time is a skill and we need to expand our conscious awareness in order to do this, and the only way to expand our conscious awareness is to judge less, moving from our immature traits into our mature, developing emotional intelligence beyond the separate self. For balance we need:

- resistance, so that we can work better with the law of polarity and with the laws of attraction;
- low vibrational emotions as a form of dense energy that we can transform into higher vibrational emotions, such as love, bliss, joy, and pleasure.

Sometimes, we will attach our heart to things that we love, and it is our attachment that creates pain and the emotional energies of anger, frustration, and passion. But *passion helps us to change the world* and sometimes, so does our anger and frustration. To have no attachment is a great thing, but if our life is lacking emotion or purpose and we don't enjoy life (as much as we feel we could), then sometimes being attached to or solving injustices in the world (environmental or social) can serve us the most, as our anger, frustration, and passion can an allow us to be the *happiest* in a balanced way and make life worth living. *Constantly raising our vibration to higher and higher levels will not always make us happy as truly embracing lower ones,* and will often create unbalance. When we have attachment, our vibration cannot go as high, but in solving injustices, in living to serve others and making the world a better place, we create balance in our life and demonstrate our free will.

The world needs balance, it needs dark and light, but as individuals and as humanity, we don't need a 50/50 equal balance. Each of us will "judge" emotional balance accordingly to our personal preferences and what we are trying to achieve: making agreements on what balance is, is impossible. Similarly, we don't need an equal balance of our masculine and feminine, mature and immature, in our internal or external expressions either, *personal imbalances are what makes each of us beautiful and unique.* What we need is multiple polarities and dualities that help to keep us all moving, changing, and eventually evolving.

Manipulation and Co-creation

As we develop a better use and understanding of polarity and duality, we need to be careful not to manipulate people, but to help them better understand themselves. This applies even more to parenting because someone is looking to us to create the structures and patterns of polarity and duality that will later guide their lives.

A healthy expression of manipulation to some people sounds impossible, but given we are learning to work with both polarity and duality in all situations, then manipulation must have a healthy expression and for this *"co-creation"* is a good fit. On one level, everything is manipulation:

- a negative intention for the other + action = manipulation;
- a positive intention for the other + action = manipulation.

You tell a joke because you want the other person to be happy and laugh, because you love them, and in its most extreme definition, this is manipulation. On an emotional level, positive and negative, do not exist as a constant, they change through time and how we judge them is determined by our desires, intention and aim. The less we rely on planning with the mind and the more we trust in our own alignment, trust in the conscious awareness that flows through us, through our physical, mental, and emotional bodies, the more we will experience freedom.

Our mind knows at times that we need to suffer to experience pain, resistance and frustration, as these help us move through duality. So, the subconscious mind chooses the pain we experience and manipulates us to get there. The sad part is that our unhealthy ego can become addicted to this pain and suffering, so we become stuck, repeating the same old patterns to detrimental effects. As our awareness increases, our relationship to good and bad, to pleasure and pain changes, our judgements change. We understand the bigger picture, so we can also take pleasure from our pain, because we know it will *later* create pleasure for us and those we love.

The subconscious mind and our ego are linked. The subconscious is more of a neutral force, acting both positively and negatively. Whereas, the unhealthy ego is mainly negative, with the healthy ego being both neutral and positive, residing in conscious awareness and acting with mindfulness (at least this is one way of several to explain the human mind). To reach the embodiment of our healthy ego, we really need to have transcended the limiting beliefs and judgements of good and bad.

By viewing and creating this polarity between our conscious and our subconscious mind in the same way, that we create the polarity between our masculine and feminine, we gain the same benefit of being able to observe, but without overly identifying as either or giving our power away, like we are victims to our subconscious and have no power or influence over it, or over ourselves.

This is not to suggest that we should start trying to *"co-create"* with other people's lives because we have a good intention for them, but it is to say that once we acknowledge and accept that many of our subconscious actions are a form of manipulation, then we can start to work with this energy in a healthier way.

Alignment = Co-creation

It's much easier to act from a place of co-creation as opposed to manipulation when we have inner alignment. For most people, but especially parents, to say that they are never consciously manipulating other adults or children to teach them something, would be a lie. But the more understanding that we can bring into a situation, admitting that we don't know it all and that with our subconscious minds we are manipulating others and ourselves all of the time, the quicker our manipulation can turn into co-creation. Accepting that we don't know everything, allows our own and the higher selves of others to work through us and to co-create with us.

We are born knowing oneness, childhood creates our separation, and growing up is the journey of reintegration.

Children need to develop their egos and there is going to be some unhealthy expressions in there. We don't need to encourage it, but we don't need to fix it either, most of the time all we need to do is to give the child the opposite mature to their immature behaviour and allow them to demonstrate their mature.

The immature masculine is hard-pressed to stay angry towards the mature feminine. And the immature feminine cannot stay in her shell of isolation when the mature masculine is present. These fundamental concepts need to be applied to all aspects of parenting. Over-emphasizing the opposing mature polarity to a teenager's immature is a great way to curb rebellion, but sometimes so is over-emphasizing the immature, manipulating (or co-creating) teenagers to act from their mature.

Again, there is no right or wrong, and it's in bringing up children that the line between manipulation and co-creation can become very thin. Your urge might be to relate to a teenager unconsciously from your immature because you're scared for their future, so you want to dominate them or take their power away until you feel safe. But by fully trusting that what happens in their life is right for them, we give them the greatest chance for success.

By finding the unhealthy personality traits and behaviours within ourselves, often created as children, through:

- concisely moving into separation and polarization,
- to develop depth and greater understanding of our immature,
- which then allows us to integrate the new depths and understanding into both our poles as one whole person,

we become more of a whole person.

Inner Child Work

It is important to note that our immature is *not* our inner child. Inner child work and shadow work often sit closely together, and depending on the type of therapy we choose, reintegrating our personality often means healing our inner child and changing our mental patterns from before the age of around eight, before trauma created so many splits in our personality.

Our inner child does not fit into boxes so well, it is genderless and exists in all the quadrants of the Masculine and Feminine Polarity Framework, and none of them. It brings a sense of innocence to any situation. Our inner child naturally accepts and trusts implicitly. It is the metaphoric beginning and the end of every journey, birth to death, thus rebirth.

The inner child is our wisest of words and our most auspicious of moments. There is no one specific concept or therapy that can fully convey inner child work. Working with our inner child every day, finding moments to be playful, innocent and to tap into our innate wisdom is key. Bringing joy, laughter, and silliness into life also helps us to see the absurdity and the beauty of it all, the wisdom and humour of the mature masculine, the auspiciousness and creativity of the mature feminine. We can all benefit from spending time with and giving space to our inner child daily, who will refuse to let you put them into boxes or onto the polarity framework anyway.

Part 5

INTEGRATIVE HEALING

50
Healing through Polarity

Integrative Healing

Integrative Healing from a non-dual perspective, the perspective of programming non-duality into the body so we do not resist pain and attach to pleasure, is a way to expand human consciousness and the human experience, and is much more than integrating our trauma and life experiences for a balanced life, although this is a very worthy thing to do: by practicing integrative healing from a non-dual mindset we are following a truly holistic practice because everything already is at one and not recognized as separate—Masculine and Feminine are not recognized as separate. We learn to integrate more dimensions and layers of life and how to weave through them in a multi-dimensional fashion that allows us to expand polarity and not be reduced by it or reductionist thinking while utilizing reductionist thinking.

We train ourselves to see that the physical, mental, emotional and energetic layers of our being are all in relationship with one another and are all affected by space and time differently, by light and dark. It's by learning to multi-task, to work multi-dimensionally that we can create enough awareness to help another see the interconnected patterns within their personal issues and the potential solutions.

To repeat the previous contradictory quotes: Einstein taught us that you cannot solve a problem with the same level of thinking that was used to create it, and Rumi says the cure for the pain is the pain. Both are true and the polarity framework shows us that when we stop focusing on what hurts, be it in our emotional or physical bodies but focus on what that pain is connected to and how else it manifests in our other bodies, then holistic and integrative development naturally occurs and our pain reduces or heals completely: but the root issue, the lesson the pain teaches us is still the focus, is still the cure, so both Einstein and Rumi are correct. When healing integratively and using the polarity framework the more contradicting truths that we can encompass to support our inner alignment, the quicker the process works and the quicker we become better, happier versions of ourself.

So to teach only breath, or only polarity, emotional release, shadow work or how to generate kundalini energy in a reductionist way would be doing a disservice to those you teach and would not fully integrate. Because of this, this book focuses on polarity and duality (or non-duality) as an essential part of the whole that we must learn in relation to the whole, but for the integrative and embodied experience of this work we need to have the experience through physical and emotional embodiment practices, so you still must go and seek these and have the experiences, only reading is not enough to understand integrative healing: you have to experience it.

Healing through Polarity

By creating splits and polarities within ourselves, it's much easier for us to heal and then reintegrate as the whole person that we are. Recognizing different parts of our self from a reductionist perspective, can teach us a lot. A reductionist perspective can never be the truth, but a momentary truth that contributes to:

- our separate experience of life;
- and our oneness and integration.

Self-love is far more achievable for most people when we separate our masculine and feminine polarities, this method of working is also one of the quickest ways out of self-hate. If we are sitting with an inner sense of hate, we can separate this part of ourselves and know that it's not who we are, but just a temporary experience of who we are. Even if we hate our masculine and/or our feminine, or our mother and/or our father, the polarity framework, used with masculine and feminine dialogue work, allows us to start the conversation that leads us to healing and transforming ourselves. It then becomes much easier to work with hate to:

- transform it;
- heal;
- and integrate it.

Generally, we will do these three things at the same time within our different bodies. The more we grasp a 5th-dimensional understanding of working with our three main bodies, in that our emotional body is not limited by time and space in the same way that our mind is, the quicker the concept of the three main bodies becomes our default point of view, and the quicker we learn to see all three of our bodies on the polarity framework.

As well as integrating our masculine and feminine polarities into an ever-increasing sense of wholeness and oneness, we are also looking for integration and alignment between our emotional, mental, and physical bodies, between the physical 3rd, 4th, and 5th dimensions. For the most part, we are healing each of these bodies through the laws of polarity and duality, vibration and attraction, and then finding alignment between them:

It is through polarity and duality, vibration and attraction, that we raise our vibration to a greater understanding of life and how the universe works.

Integrative healing allows us a safe space to emphasize and look at our dark side and our shadow, understanding their polarities, the lessons they are teaching us, thus harnessing their gifts but always reintegrating our polarities in a healthy way. By always looking for the polarization of our masculine and feminine parts and their different traits, and then integrating them, we are walking a path of both self-love and acceptance, and self-realization.

51
Masculine and Feminine Integrative Therapy Techniques

Masculine and Feminine Polarity Work is a physiological framework. It can be used alone as a self-development tool, or alongside many different therapy practices. The integrative therapy techniques that I use the most are:

1 Masculine & Feminine dialogue work: a non-dualistic adaption of a method used in Gestalt therapy, that helps us to develop emotional intelligence, developed in my private practice.

2 De-armouring: a range of physical bodywork, breathwork, and energy-work techniques that focus on the transformation of emotional information that we store in our physical bodies on the cellular level.

3 Breathwork and breath therapy: an array of breathing practices and techniques that change our way of being, approach to life, and approach to breath, while supporting us to reprogramme our cells with new information.

4 And Energetic bodywork: I work privately and teach groups to work with the human energetic field and different polarities in the body. It relates to Eastern Kundalini science, in the rising of masculine and feminine energies to gain greater self-understanding. In "Kundalini Bodywork" we teach the non-dual concepts of this book to the body instead of the mind. Although I provide structure and guidance when teaching, I believe that each therapist should be encouraged to find their own best way when it comes to energetic and kundalini bodywork, my way is East meets West and undogmatic, but yours may be different.

These four main techniques and the polarity framework are a powerful approach to transform fear, pain, and trauma, on the cellular level and to align our three bodies, so that we can live and function from a higher vibration with more access to our power.

Pain and fear are vibrations that get stuck in the cells of our physical body and act as armour. As long as our body remembers what hurt us in the past, it means we can protect ourselves from it and not get hurt again in the future. Whether a dog bit us, or a loved one left us, the memory of the pain stored in our bodies on an energetic level is the same. It's there to protect us from being hurt again, from being bitten by a dog, burning ourselves or feeling like our heart's been broken.

For most of us, around 90% of the traumas stored in our bodies are useless. The armour protects us from nothing and actually creates more of what we do not want or like in our life. By resisting jealousy; loss; abandonment; fear; anger; depression, or rage, we are being a vibrational match for them, thus, they are created in our life. Having these traumas stored in our body, means we become a self-fulfilling prophecy.

The armour simply lowers our vibration. It makes us heavy and dense, less sensitive to touch, to pleasure, and to pain. Learning to:

- not let negative vibrations become stuck in the body;
- de-armour ourselves;
- and reprogram ourselves is something that we all can do.

When using integrative therapy techniques in this way, we are healing holistically and finding alignment to access our power. So, unless our trauma is crippling, then using the physical practices on their own, and without the mental polarity framework, is not recommended. Pain and trauma are here to teach us something, so please make sure that you have understood the concepts of this book and can use the polarity framework before moving too deeply into integrative therapy techniques, especially without a trained therapist *(which is not recommended)*. It's important to heal our physical, mental, and emotional bodies together if we want to evolve consciousness.

Often, it's not one before the other, and it's through the process of de-armouring that we learn and have the realizations as to what our pain is actually about, what it is teaching us, and what we need to change.

Many people, and therapists, clear blockages and traumas from the body without checking to see if they are resolved in the mind, but from an integrative perspective, this is not wise.

Working with a trained therapist is normally always useful, but self-practice and attending workshops and trainings for self-development can also be very rewarding.

Shaking

De-armouring, breathwork, and energetic bodywork in masculine and feminine integrative therapy, means learning how:

- to shake;
- to breathe while relaxed with sound;
- to use the muscles in our pelvic floor to move energy;
- to flow energy through the masculine energy pathways of the body;
- to flow energy through the feminine energy pathways of the body;
- all of this relates to more Kundalini energy moving through us: healing, transforming, and expanding conscious awareness.

These are basic and foundational skills that allow us to release trauma and develop the emotional intelligence of our glands through bodywork.

In the next pages you will learn the basics of:

- Shaking in neutral
- Shaking in the masculine
- Opening the hips
- Shaking in the feminine
- Osho Kundalini shaking and the Taoist Microcosmic orbit

Video instructions of these exercises can also be found by following the links from www.kundalinibodywork.com to the paid for online course, or in the free content section on YouTube.

Shaking in Neutral

1 Stand hip-width apart, knees slightly bent, so you cannot see your feet, but you can see your toes. Tuck your tail bone in.

2 Now bounce on your knees in a gentle but energetic rhythm. Let the bounce come from your hips. Feel your hips, put conscious awareness into your hips, pelvis, groin, sexual organs and stomach.

3 Make sure your heels stay flat on the ground. Lifting the feet off the floor is a sign of wanting to escape the body. Stay grounded and rooted.

4 As you bounce up and down, relax the whole body, and drop the shoulders back. Open the mouth, and relax the jaw.

5 Now breathe deeply through the nose, all the way into the belly, and out through the mouth.

6 As you breathe out through the mouth, imagine you have lips on your throat, and breathe out through these lips. This relaxes the whole body, and massages the thorax and thyroid gland.

7 You should hear a soft, arrr sound on the out-breath, but make sure you are not *saying* "arrr". You should simply relax, so natural sounds arise.

8 Now keep relaxing, allowing the body to breathe, shake, and make sound.

Shaking in the Masculine

1 As we bounce up and down in neutral, we create chaos and polarity in our etheric field, the electromagnetic field that surrounds our body. We can use this field to draw more energy, chi, prana, and life force, into our body.

2 There is a soft area between our legs, called the perineum. For men, this is between our testicles, and anus, and for women, our Yoni (vagina) and anus. We also have a soft area on the crown of our head, called the anterior fontanelle. It's the last part of our skull to form, approximately twelve to eighteen months after birth.

3 Earth energy: chi, prana, and life force comes in through the perineum. And divine energy (chi, prana, life force) through the crown of the head.

4 As we tense, and hold our sexual muscles that are around and in front of our perineum, the sphincter in our anus, and our PC (pubococcygeus) muscle, which is in the middle of these two, but up deeper inside the body, we should try to fully relax the rest of the body. It's much better if we can tense these three muscles while relaxing the abdominals, unlike in most yoga postures. More energy will be able to come into our body this way. Don't worry if you cannot do

it straightaway, it takes practice, and often deep de-armouring of the pelvic floor and abdominals is needed. To begin with, you can just tense all the muscles in your pelvic floor.

5 Either way, we will start to pull energy into our body through the perineum, and this starts to give us access to our energy and power.

6 When shaking in the masculine, this energy travels through the masculine energetic pathway. Which is up the spine, to the top of our head, circling around in our head several times (if you have an advanced practice, touch your tongue to the tip of your mouth to make a circuit), and then this energy flows down our body, slightly in or slightly out of the body, and we store this energy in our naval, or lower dantian.

7 As we bounce up and down, relaxing the whole body and holding the sphincter in the anus and the PC muscle tight, our whole spine becomes erect, and we can relax our body. We can relax so much that we would do a back bend if the base of our spine was not held so tightly. The contraction of the pelvic floor without the abdominals, allows everything else to just relax, apart from our knees and ankles, so we do not fall over.

8 As we breathe like this, and pull energy and life force into our body, we are able to release old stuck energy, recent negative emotions, and micro-traumas. When we don't have fresh energy, we don't want to let go of the old, even when it's full of trauma. The moment we do not have Chi, flowing through us, is the moment we are dead. So, it makes sense that we prefer to let go when we have fresh Chi, fresh life force, but energy is infinite and abundant, and a free flow and circulation of energy throughout our body is best.

9 This is a great exercise to do in the morning and after times of stress. Don't forget to let your body make sound.

Opening the Hips

1 This exercise is not masculine or feminine. It helps us open the hips, and get more energy flowing through the spine. It's a great warm up for shaking in the feminine.

2 Place your hands either side of the body, and imagine that they are attached to your hips. Wherever your hands move, your hips move. Your hands cannot go further forward than your hips. Now roll your hips backwards.

3 The movement looks like a wave in the ocean, with four pivot points. One in the hips, two in the spine, and one in the neck, tilting the neck back on the full inhale, and returning down on the exhale.

4 Breathe deeply and powerfully in through the mouth. Really feel the air rushing through your throat. As you breathe in, your wave moves upwards, and as you breathe out through the mouth, it rolls down.

5 The roll should come from the lower spine, lumbar region. Not the knees. The knees move a little but it's the hips moving the knees. If you're finding this movement difficult then try thrusting your hips back and forth a few times, keeping your knees relatively still, and then turn this into a backwards, up-and-over, rolling movement.

6 Now as you breathe in, squeeze your PC muscle, sexual organs, and anus sphincter, and relax your abdominal muscles (if you can relax them at the same time). As you breathe in feel and imagine energy running up your spine. This energy can take some time to build, and it's hard for it to clean your spine on its own. But if your spine is clear, then this energy will feel as if it comes out the top of your head. If it does not, don't worry, just practise the movement and get the pelvic muscles used to working.

Shaking in the Feminine

1 The feminine energy pathway runs the opposite way to the masculine. It comes out from our navel or lower dantian, and up the body. Maybe slightly in, or slightly out of the body, or both. This energy travels up, and circles in the head (again if you have an advanced practice then touch the tip of your tongue to the roof of your mouth) and then it goes down the spine, out the tailbone, between the legs and back up the body, into the navel, or lower dantian.

2 There is no right or wrong way to shake in the feminine. As long as you follow the basic structure, whatever you do will be okay. The feminine likes to change her mind, and it's the diversity that brings pleasure into the body. Everybody's feminine is different and changes, the most important thing is that you find the movement that is right for you at the time. Stay relaxed and loose.

3 You can breathe in and out of the nose, or in through the nose, and out through the mouth.

4 Start with something between the neutral bounce and the hip-opening wave, which helps to bring the energy up.

5 In the masculine we pull the energy into the body, but in the feminine, we simply surrender and allow. The more we surrender to our body, to our breath, and to the movement, the more energy flows through us. It is as if we are surrendering to our own masculine energy.

6 As we move the hips and breathe, we can pulse (tense and let go, tense and let go) the pelvic floor muscles. As we pump or pulse these muscles energy is drawn up into the body. But again, we need to fully relax the rest of the body, and surrender. This difference, between surrender and resistance can be a subtle one, especially if we are tensing and releasing the muscles at the same time. Try to find more freedom in your body. Moving how you want to move. Maybe your hips go side-to-side, maybe your chest starts to bump out, or your neck rolls. Just keep coming back to a loose wave-like movement, so the energy flows up.

7 If we de-armour the pelvic floor, then these muscles can start to work on their own. When we want more energy, the pelvic floor will simply pump, without us needing to think about it.

8 For female practitioners, this exercise can be modified to use with a Yoni egg. And for male practitioners, modified exercises can help the separation of ejaculation and orgasm.

9 Everybody finds their own way to pump on the in-breath, the out-breath, or both. It might be many fast short inhales with multiple pumps, or one slow breath with a single pump. It's good to keep changing it, or letting it change as the body wants.

10 When we shake like this in our feminine, we can find our energetic blockages, and ways around them. Ultimately, we want to take them away so that we have a clear flow of energy throughout. But to start, it's good to get used to running pleasurable energy through the body. Noting where the blocks are, and applying more pumps and wave-like motions to move around them.

Osho Kundalini Shaking and the Taoist Microcosmic Orbit

1 Shaking in the masculine and shaking in the feminine, is very similar to the ancient "Taoist Microcosmic Orbit Meditations", and the more recent "Osho Kundalini Shaking". Both of these practices support each other, so it's great to try them both if you have time. Shaking in the masculine and feminine is a quick system with great effects on its own, practicing it will benefit any Kundalini shaking, or Microcosmic orbit practice. It has many similar benefits to the two named disciplines, as well as some of its own. It can be practised with or without music, and really helps in purifying and aligning our energy systems.

2 The Taoist Microcosmic Orbit uses the same masculine and feminine pathways of energy in the body, and is a base for many amazing and powerful Taoist practices.

3 Osho Kundalini Shaking is a way of fully relaxing and being in the body. Allowing breath and a certain type of music to move and shake the body. We don't shake the body, we allow the music to shake our body, and our energy rises.

4 For recommendations of music to shake to, please visit www.kundalinibodywork.com and follow the links or search for the famous "Osho Kundalini shaking music".

However you choose to practise, I hope you shake, breathe deeply and make sound every day.

Epilogue

If you've enjoyed reading this book, I'd ask you to take a few moments more to read this final chapter. These are my suggestions and practical steps for how we create an abundant, happy, technologically, and spiritually advanced society. This is not my area of expertise, but in my heart it feels right to express it here, separate to the focus of this book.

As expressed, personal and planetary transformation have to come together, similarly to how the mature feminine comes before the masculine, and mothering comes before fathering. When personal transformation is not reflected by the collective or community, then the individual is unlikely to sustain their changes, thus devolving into their immature and shadow expressions.

To see balanced mature masculine and feminine *leadership*, one of the most powerful things that we can all do is to lead with our consumer power, our energy expressed as money, by committing to or at least aiming to commit to these two statements:

"I will only spend and invest money into products and companies that are committed to creating an ethical, sociable, and sustainable world."
and
"I will not spend money where I would not want to work or see my loved ones working."

These two statements might seem radical and even unachievable, especially the last one, but to truly change collective systems and collective consciousness, change has to come from the individual's free will: the power of billions of people freely and willingly choosing the same thing, choosing to love the rest of humanity as they should love themselves. Governments and corporations control and regulate us with the power that we give them, but for healthy change on the collective level, individual change has to come first and it has to come from the heart.

Trying to organize people around anything more complicated than a statement, an idea or a belief is often too complex to implement. The above two statements are somewhat flawed and we could argue for days a better action to get this message across, but at the end of the day, we each have individual choice and should demonstrate this when we see a better way. Some days we may still want to fly on planes, buy a mobile phone or a car, and we should probably still do these things; it's important to enjoy our life and live without restriction, but the two statements are saying that: *We should aim to only give our energy, our money, to the companies who invest well into our communities and planet and send the rest bankrupt.*

Maybe we don't know or directly love anyone who wants to be a hairdresser, a lawyer, or sweep the streets, but when choosing anyone in these professions, we should be ensuring that each person we engage with or employ, directly or indirectly, has a good quality of life, understanding that their experience of consciousness affects and is our experience of consciousness. So please stop giving power away to governments and corporations and making this their job, it's time to take our power back and take responsibility for where our money goes, where our energy is going and what it is creating.

The strategy is that if enough people adopt these two statements, to the best of their ability, society will be forced into a positive and dramatic change. Many people say that an economic crash is inevitable, but a crash created slowly by ethical consumer power would be a low impact economic crash, giving us time to change the direction of industry: it will still create a rise in unemployment as we realize that so many modern-day jobs, products, and services, fulfil no other need than to keep the mass population busy and the economy turning.

Simply keeping busy is not a good thing, especially when it stops democracy working by reducing the time people have to self-govern and direct their leadership, and also the time people have for self-development and pleasure.

With enough good leaders in power, governmental and corporation leaders, who can act from their hearts with their brain, while not denying the reality and darker side of human nature, it will be possible to turn a rise in unemployment into a positive. Corporations and governments will be forced to adapt, creating an approach to time management and the distribution of wealth, giving us *all* more free time, balancing out the mass unemployment with lower working hours for most people, while ending a great number of meaningless and soul-destroying jobs, freeing people to be happy and to do what they love.

All of this needs to happen slowly enough for our governments and capitalism to adjust. One of the first steps of transition could be ensuring that profit can only be found in conscious and green companies, meaning that all forms of capitalism become conscious and green. This is the fundamental law of "supply and demand" that our economy is built on. So, for as much as your budget will allow, and it really is for the middle class to lead the way, as for the poor this can almost be impossible, and the rich are too few to count, please commit to these two statements:

"I will only spend and invest money into products and companies that are committed to creating an ethical, sociable, and sustainable world."
and
"I will not spend money where I would not want to work, or see my loved ones working."

Please feel free to write these two statements down if it helps you to commit to them.

We need systems and technology in place to support our collective and individual shifts and creativity, as without structures and an environment that supports our transformation, we are likely to fall back and devolve. When governments enforce the correct policy and tax changes within an acceptable transition period, society will change, but governments can only enforce these policies when the demos (the population) is a reflection of the changes, thus can attract them, and are a match for them.

We have to become a vibrational match for the leadership that we want, governments and corporations cannot save us in the way that many hope, we can only save ourselves.

"If we could change ourselves, the tendencies in the world would also change." – Mahatma Gandhi (1869 to 1948).

The first steps might be small and to drastically change our whole life overnight is not possible for many, but if you don't want to be a pizza delivery boy, don't call them *all the time* and don't fall into the *mental* trap of *"oh well, everyone needs work and money."* If you don't want to work in factories for the rest of your life, *aim* (you might fail sometimes, and that's okay, but aim) to only buy items that come with a 10+ year or lifetime guarantee *(just avoid cheap plastic crap at all costs)*. If you personally would not want to, or would not want your children to work in an abattoir (animal slaughter house), on a Mexican shrimp trawler, or on the conveyer belt of a frozen fish factory, please consider taking animal products out of your diet, or at least invest into plant-based nutrition and agriculture.

Important note: Plant-based diets are far more sustainable, for a far greater number of people than we are led to believe. Plant-based agricultural and nutritional practices are massively lacking because the pharmaceutical industry and modern agricultural industries, who are supposed to look after our health, are far too profitable to change to better systems of food production and health care. Thus, we are missing the investments needed in science, technology, and agriculture to make plant-based diets work on a larger scale.

Life can be beautiful for every human being on this planet for the majority of their life span, when we change the way we live.

To create such a system, change, diversity, and creativity are key. Creating a system that empowers people, allows them to lead, be creative, and integrate back into the greater whole is essential. It is not capitalism and it is not communism, it is something that we have not created yet, and it will not happen overnight; changes to our current systems and education have to come first. So, if you are a person, or represent a business, or institution who would like to get ready for and support balanced masculine and feminine leadership in our world, I highly recommend adopting these three systems:

1 Spiral Dynamics
To develop opposing human value systems to a point of integrative understanding.

2 Sociocracy, Holacracy, or similar
Unbiased and cultureless decision-making structures that take the best of autocratic, democratic, and consensus decision-making, and management styles. Once these methods are applied into child education, meaning the child gets to lead their own education, in a mixed-age setting, within a set of rules and structures, and the power of consent with their authorities, we will be raising a generation capable and ready of creating the societal, system and cultural changes needed.

3 Permaculture
Primarily, a nature-based system for land management, the principles also relate to systems of human design, following the patterns, principles,

and wisdom inherent in nature (on a more reductionist level, this is called biomimicry).

Educating people and children in systems like the above is essential to be ready for the larger collective changes that will span multiple value systems and cultures.

I hope this last chapter has encouraged you to make some positive and substantial changes in your life, alongside the ones you generate from within by using the polarity framework to evolve yourself, your masculine, your feminine, your shadow and your integrated self.

This book can work like a programme or a download, so if you start applying polarity and duality into your life now, it will become second nature and you will use it without thinking, and continue to do so for as long as you periodically review the four maps. To continue your journey please visit www.polaritywork.com and

- discover more integrative therapy practices;
- attend a workshop or online course;
- like, follow, and share on social media;
- sign up to the newsletter;
- leave a review.

With loving kindness,
Elliott Saxby

Glossary

Below are some of the major terms discussed in this book. Elsewhere you might find terms like subconscious and unconscious used interchangeably, or different definitions for consciousness, the subconscious, and unconscious.

Aligned integrated self. When feelings of unhealthy conflict dissolve, leaving a healthy balance of masculine and feminine that allows our higher self to act through us.

Bad. Often a judgement and preference dictated by the circumstances and desires of a person.

Collective intelligence/consciousness. The conscious awareness of a group or collective. From small groups of people to large groups of people, people who know each other and people who do not. Your conscious mind, your subconscious, your consciousness and your higher self are all connected to a range of different collective intelligences which inform what you think, feel and how you act, as well as what your intuition picks up on.

Compersion. To feel joy for another's joy.

Conscious Mind. What we are consciously aware of on the mental level.

Consciousness, or conscious awareness. Our ability to project our awareness from our mind to other parts of our body and outside of our body. To feel our emotions, to develop empathy for another person, to be conscious of what others feel and experience. To expand our awareness is to make the unconscious conscious.

Duality. The reflection of a spectrum.

Emotional body is 5th-dimensional. It is beyond time and space. The emotional body and intuition are experienced as 5D. A multidimensional reality with different realities interrelating and affecting one another. It is beyond full comprehension with a 4D mind. But for the emotional body, logic, and linearity do not matter. It does not matter if the event happened to you or someone else, if it's past, future, present, or even in someone else's past. For the emotional body truth is belief.

Good. Often a judgement and preference dictated by the circumstances and desires of a person.

Healthy. The natural and optimal state, physically, mentally and emotionally. Desirable and satisfactory.

Healthy ego. Liberated sense of "I", allows us to experience separation without the fear or denial of oneness. Expressions of our personality arise from mindfulness and actions, as opposed to trauma and reactions.

Higher self. A part of the self that vibrates at a much higher frequency, taps into the unconscious, and feeds us information from outside of ourselves. It partly lives in the collective consciousness and when life flows perfectly, and with synchronicity, this is our higher self working through us. The higher self can be experienced in many different ways, as it acts in a multi-dimensional fashion, serving multiple purposes. Different people define our higher self in different ways, I find it is best to avoid a definitive definition because it holds multiple truths and expresses itself in multiple ways.

As you come to a more 5th-dimensional understanding of life, it becomes easier to allow multiple truths to exist at the same time without a need of permanent classification. Creating better communication with our higher self allows us to understand the various abstractions towards oneness and what is relevant to our here and now, to creating more life and beauty here and now. Making good use of the polarity framework and working with the integrative therapy techniques to have better access to our emotions and intuition, will give both better alignment and better communication with our higher self.

Immature. Not fully developed, often acting from fear, sometimes childlike, naïve, and crude. Can be healthy or unhealthy.

Integrated self. Our outer expression to the world; generally, a mix of our shadow, immature, and mature self.

Inner Masculine and Inner Feminine. Both men and women have a masculine and a feminine, they exist separate from gender, although stereotypically men tend to be in their masculine more often, and women in their feminine.

Intuition. This is often felt in the stomach and for women also the womb, but it actually has no physical location. It is on par with the higher self, but transmits the collective intelligence and unconscious into our consciousness. To work with our intuition, we need to trust ourselves and have an open heart. The more we trust our intuition, the more it works.

Mature. A constantly deepening stage of mental and emotional development. Can be healthy or unhealthy.

Mental body is 4th-dimensional. It works in a linear time frame. 'A' happens and then 'B' happens.

Paradox. A concept that changes each time you understand it, due to your understanding.

Physical body is 3rd-dimensional. Always in the present moment, always in the now. For the physical body, there is no time. It is always now. Like a static 3D object or still photograph.

Polarity. Two opposite ends of a spectrum.

Separate self. Our experience of the world from the mind. Reacting to the world from our memories and mental programming, without access to empathy, emotional intelligence, and the collective consciousness.

Shadow. Extremely unhealthy immature with no obvious healthy side. It allows us to recognize light and gives us a direction in which to move. Recognizing our shadow is recognizing our fears, seeing the helpfulness of them and how they serve us. When our evolution is stuck, we can use our shadow as a greater level of polarity. A polarity that moves life forward. When we are unconsciously acting from our shadow, we are simply acting from fear.

Subconscious Mind. The part of our mind which we are not fully aware of and which influences our actions and feelings. The more awareness we bring to our subconscious mind, the more we understand ourselves. The subconscious mind also creates the shadow aspects of our personality from suppressed fears, desires and similar. The subconscious mind is a semi-conscious part of our being, to an extent we can programme it to change our behaviour, but for the most part, it acts more independently than we give it *(ourselves)* credit for.

The Inner Child. A psychological concept that changes depending on what you need, based on the theory that we all have an inner child inside of us.

The Unconscious. All the knowledge of the universe that we are yet to become conscious of. All that we do not know and are unconscious of. Limitless possibilities.

Unhealthy. A deformed, mutated, and unnatural state. Undesirable and non-satisfactory.

Unhealthy ego. Perpetuates separation and reactional behaviours led by the mind. Our unhealthy ego is created by and is part of our subconscious mind. It's the part of us that acts from pre-programmed beliefs. These might be good beliefs that serve us, or beliefs that come from a place of fear and hinder us.

Recommended Reading

When I was asked to create this recommended reading list I struggled as although I've now written a book there are not so many books that I've read all the way through, so it's hard to recommend some of the major authors who have influenced me. To a point this book just seemed to come into my consciousness after a lot of self-purification and a few dark nights of the soul; it was more like it was channelled or downloaded, and then refined through personal experience and the experiences of the many clients who came through my therapy practice and workshops.

As I walked out of school at 12, I'm self-taught in most topics and generally read for specific knowledge when younger, so instead of only giving a list of books I'm also giving a list of authors who have influenced me, ones that anyone who knows work similar to this book and the polarity framework, would expect to see here.

One: Essential Writings On Nonduality, by Jerry Katz.
The Quantum and the Lotus, by Matthieu Richard & Trinh Xuan Thuan.
Principles of Buddhist Tantra, by Kirti Tsenshap Rinpoche.
Sexual Healing, The Shaman Method of Sex Magic, by Baba Dez Nichols & Kamala Devi.
The Magdalen Manuscript, by Tom Kenyon and Judi Sion.
Hands of Light, by Barbara Brennan.
The Earth Care Manual, by Patrick Whitefield.
We the People, Consenting to Deeper Democracy, by John Buck and Sharon Villines.
Spiral Dynamics, by *Don Edward Beck and Prof. Christopher C. Cowan.*
A Theory of Everything, by Ken Wilber.
The Prophet, by Kahlil Gibran.
Mantak Chia (various titles)
David Deida (various titles)
Carl Jung (various titles)
Wilhelm Reich (various titles)
Rumi (various titles)
Osho (various titles)

Index

About the Author

~

Photo by Michela di Savino

Elliott Saxby was born in England and prefers to describe his childhood as more colourful than traumatic. He left home at 15 and a few years later was working for the Global Ecovillage Network and the Findhorn Foundation, an education and demonstration centre for alternative living, a community with a large Buddhist influence.

Over the years and through several different careers, he studied various body and energy work modalities at home and in Asia. His passion for healing, self-development, and expanding consciousness turned into his successful integrative therapy practice based in Zürich, Switzerland, where Masculine and Feminine Polarity Work and Kundalini Bodywork are two of the core components.

For more information about Elliott and his School of Energetic Bodyworks visit:
https://elliottsaxby.com and **www.polaritywork.com**

FINDHORN PRESS

Life-Changing Books

Learn more about us and our books at
www.findhornpress.com

For information on the Findhorn Foundation:
www.findhorn.org